Competition Law in Bosnia and Herzegovina

Competition Law in Bosnia and Herzegovina

Second Edition

Kanita Imamović-Čizmić
Zinka Grbo

This book was originally published as a monograph in the International Encyclopaedia of Laws/Competition Law.

Founding Editor: Roger Blanpain†
General Editor: Frank Hendrickx
Volume Editors: Francesco Denozza & Alberto Toffoletto

Wolters Kluwer

Published by:
Kluwer Law International B.V.
PO Box 316
2400 AH Alphen aan den Rijn
The Netherlands
E-mail: lrs-sales@wolterskluwer.com
Website: www.wolterskluwer.com/en/solutions/kluwerlawinternational

Sold and distributed by:
Wolters Kluwer Legal & Regulatory U.S.
920 Links Avenue
Landisville, PA 17538
United States of America
E-mail: customer.service@wolterskluwer.com

Printed on acid-free paper

ISBN 978-94-035-6360-2

e-Book: ISBN 978-94-035-6370-1
web-PDF: ISBN 978-94-035-6380-0

The Authors

Kanita Imamović-Čizmić was born in Zenica (Bosnia and Herzegovina) in 1973. She graduated from the Law Faculty of the University of Sarajevo in 1999. Since 2012, she has been holding the position of Assistant Professor at the Law and Economics Department of the Faculty. She teaches Competition Law and Policy as well as Law of Economic System and Law of Economic System in Europe. Dr Kanita Imamović-Čizmić obtained her PhD at the Sarajevo University Faculty of Law in 2012. The title of the doctoral dissertation was 'The modalities of legal regulation of market competition and their use in the economy of Bosnia and Herzegovina.' She participated in many conferences and is an author of a number of scientific articles in the field of competition law and policy of which can be extracted:

'The starting premise in the modeling of legal regulation of competition in the less developed countries' Annual of the Faculty of Law in Sarajevo, 2008th, 'Macroeconomic Aspect of Competition Law enforcement – Review from BiH', International Conferences of The School of economic and business in Sarajevo, October 2010, 'Dual nature of institute of fairness in competition law', 'Overview', Journal of Social Issues, 2010th, 'International Conference ICES 2012' 'Beyond the Economics Crisis: Lessons Learned and Challenges Ahead' 12–13 October 2012th, Sarajevo, Bosnia and Herzegovina, Conference topic indication: 'Law and Economics' Title of the paper: 'Institutional precondition of legal protection of market competition in Bosnia and Herzegovina.' Modalities of legal regulation of competition and their relationship with the economic role of the state, Annual of the Faculty of Law in Sarajevo, 2012th, 'Hart-Scott-Rodino Act and Concentration in the American Modality of Legal Regulation of Market Competition' Annual of the Faculty of Law in Sarajevo, 2013th, 'Legal protection of market competition in the telecommunications sector in European Union lessons for Bosnia and Herzegovina', International scientific conference on the topic: Legal and economic aspects of integration process of Bosnia and Herzegovina in the European Union, Economic faculty Mostar, Law Faculty Mostar, November 2013th. 'Competition advocacy in BiH', 'Overview,' University of Sarajevo, 2014th. She is an author of the book 'Market competition protection mechanism in Bosnia and Herzegovina', Lambert Academic Publishing, 2014th.

The Authors

Zinka Grbo was born in Sarajevo (Bosnia and Herzegovina) in 1976. She graduated from the Law Faculty of the University of Sarajevo in 1999. Since 2013, she has been holding the position of an Associate Professor at the Civil Law Department of the Faculty. She teaches Company Law as well as Business Law and European Business Law. She earned her PhD degree in 2007 at the Law Faculty of the University of Sarajevo by defending her doctoral thesis, 'Public Procurement in Comparative Law.' She had been engaged as an assistant/ professor at the School of Economics, Faculty of Traffic and Communication and Academy of Performing Arts of the University of Sarajevo. She was a fellow at the University of Richmond School of Law in Richmond, VA (USA) as a Junior Fellow Development Program's participant sponsored by the United States Government. She is an appointed arbitrator at the List of Arbitrators of the Arbitration Centre attached to the Chamber of Commerce of Bosnia and Herzegovina. She is a member of the International Court of Arbitration of the International Chamber of Commerce (ICC).

Table of Contents

Table of Contents

List of Abbreviations

BiH	Bosnia and Herzegovina
CBBiH	The Central Bank of Bosnia and Herzegovina
EBRD	European Bank for Reconstruction and Development
EU	European Union
FBiH	Federation of Bosnia and Herzegovina
LoC	Law on Competition
OECD	Organisation for Economic Cooperation and Development
RS	Republic of Srpska
SAA	Stabilisation and Association Agreement

List of Abbreviations

General Introduction

§1. General Background of the Country

1. Bosnia and Herzegovina (BiH) is located in the heart of Europe, more precisely on the borderline of the West and the East. Centuries ago, it had represented the line between Christian and Muslim world. Geographically, it belongs to Southeast Europe, precisely to the peninsula of the Balkans. It has been surrounded by Croatia, Serbia and Montenegro, with 20 kilometres of the Adriatic coastline in Neum.

2. Bosnia and Herzegovina is quite a small state of 19,767 square kilometres and almost 5 million inhabitants of Catholic, Orthodox and Islamic religions. There are three official languages – Bosnian, Croatian and Serbian.

3. The capital of Bosnia and Herzegovina is Sarajevo, well known as the place where the First World War started, triggered by the assassination of the Archduke Franz Ferdinand, heir to the throne of the Austro-Hungarian Empire, in the city centre on 28 June 1914. Lately, Sarajevo has been known for the 14th Winter Olympics. Unfortunately, recently, Bosnia and Herzegovina has been made famous by the bloodiest war at the end of the twentieth century.

4. Bosnia and Herzegovina is a relatively young state. It has been independent from Yugoslavia since 1992, after the famous independence referendum. The Republic of Bosnia and Herzegovina was admitted as a Member of the United Nations by General Assembly resolution in May 1992, just after the Yugoslavian Army had attacked the country, which was the beginning of the four-year war.

§2. Economic System

5. The economic system of Bosnia and Herzegovina is determined by the complicated constitutional and legal arrangement, incomplete transition and the degree of rehabilitation of the war-shattered economy and its development. The general elements of the economic system of Bosnia and Herzegovina are: the restrictive economic role of the state, constitutionally guaranteed single market of Bosnia and Herzegovina, and, following the privatisation process, private property became the recognised form of ownership of the means of production and the concept of open economy was established.

6. Bosnia and Herzegovina is a small, open and transition economy, and as such, it is very susceptible to external shocks that followed after the last global economic crisis. The Bosnian and Herzegovinian economy did not have the capacity to reduce the negative impact of the foreign trade parameters caused by the global financial crisis on its real sector. The lack of 'defensive' capacities also includes the insufficient competitiveness of the domestic production that could cope with the impact of the crisis, and the inadequate economic policy and lack of coordination in the application of monetary and fiscal tools in response to external shocks caused by the global financial crisis.

7. The basic macroeconomic indicators in 2014, which reflect the condition of the economic system in Bosnia and Herzegovina, are as follows:

- Eurozone's exit from the recession after two years of negative growth, drop in global prices, deflation and floods in the second trimester of 2014 had an impact on the modest economic growth of 0.6% in 2014.
- retail sector registered a growth of 1.7%, which is the result of increased trade in non-food products (by 7.7%) and motor fuels (by 1.5%) on the one side, and the decreased trade in food, beverages and tobacco (by 5%) on the other.
- after a steady decline in the past five years, the construction sector registered a realistic growth of 6.6% in 2014. Increased operating activities were also registered in the domain of construction engineering (by 7.3%) and civil engineering (by 5.6%), and judging by everything, this increase took place within the rise of both private and public investments.
- the industrial sector registered a stagnation of the physical volume of industrial production in 2014, with a slight growth rate of 0.1% in relation to 2013, whereby the only positive contribution to the industrial production was achieved thanks to the activities of the processing industry which, despite many challenges in 2014, has managed to register an annual growth of production of 3.8% in relation to the year before, thus influencing the increase of total BiH exports in the end of the year. This type of condition in the industrial sector came as a result of a negative growth rate of 10% in the electricity production sector, which took place after the level of production in hydropower plants and mining sector dropped by 2%.
- determinants of the situation in the labour market in Bosnia and Herzegovina are the limited geographic and professional mobility of the workforce, fragmentation of the labour market and inconsistent policy of resolving the issue of unemployment. The said determinants came as a consequence of existence of divided competences in the field of labour and employment and the complex legal system, comprised by entity and cantonal regulations which control the basic categories in the field of labour and active and passive measures on the labour market.

Compared to the countries in the European Union (EU) and region (except for Macedonia in 2014), BiH had the highest unemployment rate and it continues to register the highest unemployment rate. Average number of employed persons in BiH in 2014 increased by 1.7% and amounted to 701,617, whereby the average number of employed persons in Federation of Bosnia and Herzegovina (FBiH) amounted to 443,600, which is by 1.9% more than compared with 2013, while the average number of employed persons in Republic of Srpska (RS) amounted to 241,520 with the growth rate of 1.2%g/g. The number of employed persons increased the most in the fields of the processing industry, and in terms of FBiH, in the sector of wholesale and retail and hotel and restaurant business.

8. The fiscal system in Bosnia and Herzegovina has the characteristics of fiscal federalism, which is a direct consequence of the complex and specific arrangement of Bosnia and Herzegovina. The responsibility for conducting the fiscal policy is not mentioned in the Constitution of BiH, nor were the state authorities (Council of Ministers of BiH) assigned any role in collecting public revenues. This paradox of a state without any competences in control and collection of public revenues has produced very serious consequences on the possibility of maintaining macroeconomic stability and establishing efficient market structures. Constitutions and laws of entities and the Brcko District (which had certain fiscal autonomy), derived from the position that was assigned to them, and which had more elements of statehood than BiH itself, defined the structure of fiscal revenues.

9. The Constitution of FBiH granted the cantons a significant level of responsibility in collection and allocation of fiscal revenues. Since the state level had no competences in the control and collection of fiscal revenues, entities adopted the laws on qualification of public revenues, in agreement with the IMF, defined the customs tariffs as their own revenue and determined the entity governments as being in charge of collection, allocation and control of these funds. The tax competition between the entities and the district was concluded with a centralisation of indirect taxes at state level. The reform of the system of indirect taxes, which was launched in 2003, has brought a radical change in fiscal relations between different levels of authorities. Following the reform of indirect taxation, the high degree of mutual fiscal co-dependency of all levels of authority has raised the question of fiscal coordination between different levels of authority in BiH. Observing the structure of revenues in the consolidated budget of BiH, one can conclude that the tax revenues accounted for 89% of the structure of revenues in 2011 and that they have an important role in financing public needs.

10. Monetary policy in Bosnia and Herzegovina has its basis in Article 7 of the Dayton Constitution and has the features of a monetary committee, meaning that it is characterised by the inability to enforce basic instruments of monetary policy and immaturity in comparison with the monetary policy of the EU. Two foundations of this policy are the Central Bank and convertible mark as the currency. The Central Bank of Bosnia and Herzegovina (CBBiH) was founded on 20 June 1997 by the Law on Central Bank, which was adopted by the Parliamentary Assembly of BiH, and it launched its operations on 11 August 1997. The main characteristics of the monetary committee are reflected in several facts. The currency of Bosnia and Herzegovina, convertible mark (KM – BAM), is connected by a fixed exchange rate with the German mark (DEM). This fixed rate is KM 1 = EUR 0.51129. KM has been connected to the euro in the same currency exchange rate since 1 January

1999. Central Bank's liabilities in KM have to be fully covered by convertible foreign funds. CBBiH has to be ready to change KM to DEM at any time of the day and in any amount.[1]

§3. Legal System

11. Bosnia and Herzegovina is composed of two Entities FBiH (decentralised, composed of ten cantons) and the RS (centralised), plus the District of Brčko. The constitutional structure is asymmetric and quite complex; it means not only one, or at least three, but thirteen constitutions. At the same time, such a decentralised structure means huge administrative machinery comprises of flabbergasting number of 149 ministers.[2] Most matters are the responsibility of the entities and very few are on the state level. The following matters are the responsibilities of the institutions of Bosnia and Herzegovina: foreign policy, foreign trade policy, customs policy, monetary policy, finances of the institutions and for the international obligations of Bosnia and Herzegovina, immigration, refugee, and asylum policy and regulation, international and inter-Entity criminal law enforcement, including relations with Interpol, establishment and operation of common and international communications facilities, regulation of inter-Entity transportation and air traffic control.[3] All governmental functions and powers not expressly assigned in the Constitution of Bosnia and Herzegovina to its institutions shall be those of the Entities.[4]

12. Main areas are responsibility of the entities, and this is the reason why in Bosnia and Herzegovina, there are very few laws at state level. Above-mentioned Article 3 paragraph (3) could be considered as a disintegrating factor of (the market) Bosnia and Herzegovina. Significantly enough, although there are not many of them, all state laws[5] are in line with the *acquis*. The Constitution of Bosnia and Herzegovina[6] lowered the jurisdiction for a lot of economic matters, which is completely contrary to the sense of economic relations. Bosnia and Herzegovina is too small a country for such a decentralisation, too small for having, for example, three laws on company, two laws on obligations, three laws on bankruptcy, three real property laws.

1. https://www.cbbh.ba/CurrencyExchange/.
2. Council of Ministers of Bosnia and Herzegovina ten ministers, Republic of Srpska Government seventeen ministers, Federation of Bosnia and Herzegovina seventeen ministers, ten Cantons in Federation of Bosnia and Herzegovina ninety-nine ministers and District Brčko Government six ministers.
3. Constitution of Bosnia and Herzegovina, Art. 3(1).
4. Constitution of Bosnia and Herzegovina, Art. 3(3).
5. Such as Public Procurement Law, Competition Act, State Aid Law.
6. The Constitution of Bosnia and Herzegovina is the fourth Annex of the Dayton Peace Agreement reached in Dayton, Ohio, USA on 21 Nov. 1995 and formally signed in Paris on 14 Dec. 1995 putting an end to the Bosnian War of Independence. For this reason, the Constitution has the form of an international treaty.

13. On the other side, political determination of many factors and legal solutions is inevitable. What political decision in legal area can do and what damage can it cause?

The complex political and ethnical structure in Bosnia and Herzegovina has determined the rule by which members of the particular decision-making body are appointed primarily on the ground of their nationality. That fact by itself is already controversial, even without adding the rule by which the decision-making process is conditioned by national voting. The example of the Competition Council's composition and decision-making process speaks for itself.

14. The way of composition would not be problematic itself since it mirrored complex and rich national structure of Bosnia and Herzegovina. The problem arises when national structure is set as a parameter in deciding whether or not there is a violation of law or in establishing a (new) legal concept, as stated in the Competition Act. Decisions of the Council of Competition shall be made by majority vote of members present, provided that at least one member from among the constituent peoples must vote for each decision.[7] It is obvious and unacceptable that political and national (often nationalistic) reasons could prevail over professional and legal arguments.

15. Integration of Bosnia and Herzegovina is the leading interest for the citizens and the state, not only of Bosnia and Herzegovina but also for the states and people of the EU, as well as the EU itself. Integration into the EU is probability for Bosnia and Herzegovina to become more integrated itself.

16. At the same time, internal integration and stabilisation are a precondition for the stabilisation and improvement of the Region. Besides going through the integration process, Bosnia and Herzegovina goes through more processes like building peace, stability and democratic consolidation, which makes the situation even more complicated. Integration into the EU is a question of geopolitical and strategic nature (the 'enigma' of Bosnia and Herzegovina). That goes for Bosnia and Herzegovina more than for the other countries in Europe[8] because it means legal, political and economic stability not only for Bosnia and Herzegovina but for the Region and the EU as well.

17. Besides the political arguments, there are also economic reasons which are not enabling Bosnia and Herzegovina to get closer to the EU. As it is known, according to one of the three Copenhagen criteria, a state needs to satisfy the 'existence of functioning market economy and capacities of the economy to cope with competitive pressures and market forces in the Union'. It is possible to view the issue of the existence of functioning market economy through a few sub-criteria,[9]

---

7. Competition Act, Art. 24(2).
8. With the exception of Greece.
9. Macroeconomic stability has been achieved including adequate price stability and sustainable public finances and external accounts; broad consensus exists about the essentials of economic policy; significant barriers to market entry (establishment of new firms) and exit (bankruptcies) are absent;

while capacity to cope with competitive pressure and market forces within the Union could be questioned, whether domestic companies have enough capacities to accept these changes.

§4. Historical Background of Antitrust Law

18. Being a developing country in transition, Bosnia and Herzegovina does not have a long tradition of enforcement of antitrust law in the sense in which this law exists in developed countries such as the USA and EU Member States. This comes as a consequence of the fact that for nearly half a century, Bosnia and Herzegovina enforced the concept of command economy, meaning a model in which the market system and competition failed to perform their primary functions.

19. Essential characteristic of the legal system of the ex-Socialist Federal Republic of Yugoslavia was its socialist character. The basic form of ownership constituted after the Second World War was State ownership, while the basic instrument of economic development was an all-inclusive State plan. The ex-Yugoslav law, as a socialist self-management law, has ensured that the working class is the holder and bearer of economic and political sovereignty. The forms of ownership in ex-Yugoslav law were closely related to the socio-economic conditions which made up the essence of that social system.

20. Basic components of the ex-Yugoslav social order and organisation were the social ownership of the resources for production and the power in the hands of working people, which were manifested through a system of social self-management and the associated labour. In those kinds of socio-economic conditions, property relations were manifested through two basic forms. One of these forms was the social ownership of the totality of property relations in ex-Yugoslav law. Within the framework of that basic form of property and within its limits emerged the right of ownership of citizens and of civil law legal entities, as the second form of ownership. According to the Constitution of ex-Yugoslavia, 'social ownership of the means of production and other resources ensures that everyone becomes integrated, under equal conditions, into associated labour working with social resources and that, by realizing his right to work with social resources and on the basis of his own labour, he earns income for the satisfaction of his personal and common needs'.[10]

21. Along with the economic transition from the end of the last century and the dissolution of the Socialist Federal Republic of Yugoslavia (1992–1995), came a

---

equilibrium between demand and supply is established by the free interplay of market forces, prices, as well as trade, are liberalised; the legal system, including the regulation of property rights, is in place, laws and contracts can be enforced and the financial sector is sufficiently well developed to channel savings towards productive investment.

10. More on ex-Yugoslavian legal system in: Guide to The Yugoslav Legal System (1977), Institute of Comparative Law, Belgrade.

new stage in the development of competition law in Bosnia and Herzegovina, all within the Single Economic Space in BiH.[11]

22. Up until 2001, only certain institutes of law and competition policy regulated in an isolated and unsystematic manner several entity trade laws. With the adoption of the Law on Competition of 2001, a significant step forward was made towards the establishment of modern competition law, despite the fact that the said Law did not fully follow the European practice and solutions, even though it assumed the provisions of Articles 101 and 102 of the Treaty on the Functioning of the EU.

23. The Law on Competition of BiH (LoC)/Competition Act of Bosnia and Herzegovina, which was adopted on 29 June 2005, represents the first official legal act that followed the practice and solutions of the modern European legislation – *legal acquis* of the EU, adopted with the goal of fulfilling the obligations on the path towards European integration. LoC is for the most part aligned with the rules and regulations of the EU[12] in the field of market competition.

24. Since its adoption, the Law has been amended on two occasions. On the first occasion in 2007,[13] the deadline for issuing decision on registered concentrations of the Council of Competition was changed from three to six months. The second occasion in 2009[14] regarded three main issues. First, enhancing the 'Council of Competition' work transparency by publishing its decisions in detail in daily papers. Second, shortening the deadline for issuing decision on initiation the procedure of notification on concentration. This means that the Council of Competition, on the basis of information and documentation that are submitted with the notification of concentration, the degree of probability of violation of competition rules through such concentration, and an estimation that the intended concentration does not result in negative effects, may adopt a decision within thirty days, instead of sixty, as it had been previously regulated. Third, the concretisation of the deadline for final decision on concentration. According to this, upon adoption of decision on initiation of the proceedings, the Council of Competition shall make a final decision within:

a. six months for determination of the prohibited agreements prescribed in Article 4 of the Law on Competition;

---

11. The project Single Economic Space in Bosnia and Herzegovina as a part of CARDS programme was finished in June 2005. The main focus of this project was on three main economic areas: competitions, consumer protection and freedom of transport and industrial products safety. The main activities of this project were created with the aim to enhance to establish single economic market in Bosnia and Herzegovina, which represents a big step ahead towards European integration.
12. For example, the regulations adopted in 2003 and 2004 – statutes of the Council and Committee No. 1/2003, 139/2004, 773/2004, and 802/2004 and so on. *See*: https://bihkonk.gov.ba/en/jurisdictions/ (24 Mar. 2010).
13. 'Official Gazette BiH' No. 76/07.
14. 'Official Gazette BiH' No. 80/09.

b. three months for determination of the individual exemption prescribed in Article 5 of the Law on Competition;
c. four months for determination of abuse of dominant position prescribed in Article 11 of the Law on Competition;
d. three months for determination of the assessment of concentration prescribed in Article 18 of this Act.

Part I. Structure of Antitrust Law and Its Enforcement

Chapter 1. Sources of Antitrust Law

§1. National Sources

25. The sources of antitrust law in Bosnia and Herzegovina are as follows.

I. The Constitution of BiH

26. The Constitution of Bosnia and Herzegovina is an integral part (Annex 4) of the General Framework Agreement for Peace in Bosnia and Herzegovina (Dayton Peace Agreement), which was initialled on 21 November 1995 in Dayton, USA, and signed on 14 December 1995 in Paris, France, and which ended the tragic conflict in the region. In its form, the Dayton Peace Agreement is actually a system comprised of one framework agreement and twelve special agreements called annexes.

27. As the supreme legal act, the Constitution of Bosnia and Herzegovina does not contain a provision on the protection of market competition which would underline the importance of free and equal access to the market, in the sense of declaring null and void any activity or act whose objective and consequence is to prevent, restrict or disrupt the market competition in the relevant market of BiH.

28. The Preamble of the Constitution underlines the desire to promote general welfare and economic growth through the protection of private property and the promotion of a market economy.

29. Article 4, paragraph 4 carries the guarantee of free movement of goods, services, capital and persons. The interpretation of these provisions implies the protection of single integral market of BiH. In line with that, any activity which brings into question the said freedoms by restricting, disrupting and preventing the competition on the Bosnian and Herzegovinian market may be considered as violation of the constitutional provisions.

30. This type of interpretation of the letter of the Constitution of Bosnia and Herzegovina has never been used in practice to date.

II. Constitutions of the Entities

A. *The Constitution of the FBiH*

31. In line with Article 9(1) and (3) of the Constitution of the FBiH, the Constitutional Assembly reached a decision on 30 March 1994 to declare the Constitution of the FBiH. The Constitution of the FBiH entered into force at midnight on 30 March 1994.

32. The Constitution of the FBiH does not contain a provision that would serve to protect the market competition from actions that could disrupt, prevent or restrict it. Only the Preamble of the Constitution of FBiH underlines the desire to support individual liberty and development of free market.

B. *The Constitution of the RS*

33. The Constitution of the RS was adopted by the National Assembly of the RS and it entered into force on 28 February 1992. Unlike the Constitution of BiH and the Constitution of FBiH, the Constitution of the RS contains the norms that both indirectly and directly protect competition. This can be seen in Article 5 of the general provisions, which specifies that the constitutional organisation of the RS is based upon free market economy, while Article 52, paragraph 2 prohibits monopolies. This position is contrary to the economic theory and practice, meaning the modern legislation, which does not prohibit the existence of a dominant position based on economic principles, but its abuse, and this is the context in which it is necessary to change it.

III. Laws

34.

a. Law on Competition of BiH (LoC);[15]
b. Law on the State Aid System;[16]
c. Law on Administrative Procedure;[17]
d. Law on Trade of FBiH[18] (*lex specialis*);
e. Law on Trade of RS[19] (*lex specialis*);
f. Law on Consumer Protection of BiH;[20]

---

15. 'The Official Gazette of BiH', Nos 48/05, 76/07, 80/09.
16. 'The Official Gazette of BiH', No. 10/12.
17. 'The Official Gazette of BiH', Nos 29/02, 12/04, 88/07 i 91/09.
18. 'The Official Gazette of the Federation of BiH', Nos 64/04 i 12/05.
19. 'The Official Gazette of the Republic of Srpska', No. 6/ 07.
20. 'The Official Gazette of BiH', No. 25/06.

g. Law on Copyright and Related Rights and Law on the Collective Management of Copyright and Related Rights;[21]
h. Law on the power companies and telecommunications (Law on Electric Power, Law on Transmission of Electric Power, Regulator and System Operator in BiH, Law on Communications);
i. Laws from the field of transport (Law on Aviation, entity laws on railways, Law on Postal Service of BiH);
j. Criminal codes (state and entity level);
k. Law on Companies of FBiH,[22] Company Law of RS;[23]
l. Law on Public Enterprises in FBiH,[24] Law on Public Enterprises in RS;[25]
m. Law on Foreign Trade Policy of BiH;[26]
n. Other laws;
o. By-laws of the Council of Competition (organisational and material and legal acts, criminal policy regulations, group exemptions and similar).

In the process of enforcement of the LoC and other statutes which regulate the issues of competition, the dominating principles are the principles of *lex specialis derogat legi generali* and *lex posterior derogat legi priori.*

§2. International Sources

35. As a 'potential candidate' for full-fledged membership in the EU, Bosnia and Herzegovina has a duty to harmonise its legal system with the EU *acquis* and to properly enforce both the existing and future legislation in line with the method specified in the 'harmonisation clause' of the Stabilisation and Association Agreement (SAA).

36. From the aspect of antitrust law, the most significant provision of the SAA is contained in Article 71, paragraph 1, which under certain conditions treats agreements, abuse of dominant position and state aid as incompatible with the functioning of the SAA. Paragraph 2 of Article 71 of the SAA specifies that any practice contrary to this provision will be evaluated based on criteria which emanate from the enforcement of the rules on competition that are in place in the EU, and the instruments for interpretation adopted by the EU institutions, the European Commission and the European Court of Justice.

37. At the same time, the provision of Article 43, paragraph 7 of the LoC, leaves it to the discretion of the Council of Competition, as the body in charge of public enforcement of antitrust law, to apply the judicial practice of the European Court of

21. 'The Official Gazette of BiH', No. 63/10.
22. 'The Official Gazette of the Federation of BiH', Nos 23/99, 45/00, 2/02, 6/02, 29/03, 68/05, 91/07, 84/08.
23. 'The Official Gazette of the Republic of Srpska', No. 127/08.
24. 'The Official Gazette of the Federation of BiH', Nos 08/05, 81/08.
25. 'The Official Gazette of the Republic of Srpska', No. 75/04.
26. 'The Official Gazette of BiH', No. 7/98.

Justice and decisions of the European Commission for the purpose of assessing the case in question. The provision of Article 71, paragraph 2 of the SAA, has set a higher standard in this matter because it demands mandatory assessment of the case before the national bodies in charge of protecting the competition law based on judicial practice of the European Court of Justice and the decisions of the European Commission to the extent in which it can have an impact on the trade between the EU and BiH.

38. In 2005, the Council of Competition of BiH became a member of the International Competition Network, and in this aspect, it is important to underline the enforcement of the Guidelines and recommendations of this international forum, as well as those adopted by the Organisation for Economic Cooperation and Development (OECD).

§3. Secondary Sources

I. Regulations

39. Article 25 of the LoC regulates the competence to enact by-law acts in a way that the Council of Competition is competent to enact by-laws, and in that sense, the secondary sources are:

1. Regulation on the Procedure for Granting Immunity from Fines (Leniency Policy).[27]
2. Regulation on Notification and Criteria for the Assessment of a Concentration of Undertakings.[28]
3. Regulation on Annexes and Amendments to Agreements of Minor Importance.[29]
4. Regulation on the Definition of a Relevant Market.[30]
5. Regulation on Agreements of Minor Importance.[31]
6. Regulation on Block Exemption Granted to Certain Categories of Horizontal Agreements (Between Undertakings Operating on the Same Level of Production or Distribution Chain) Relating Particularly to Research, Development and Specialisation Agreements.[32]
7. Regulation on Block Exemption Granted to Certain Categories of Technology Transfer Agreements (Licence and Know-how Agreements).[33]
8. Regulation on Block Exemption Granted to Insurance Agreements.[34]

27. 'The Official Gazette of BiH', No. 34/10.
28. 'The Official Gazette of BiH', No. 34/10.
29. 'The Official Gazette of BiH', No. 34/10.
30. 'The Official Gazette of BiH', No. 18/06.
31. 'The Official Gazette of BiH', No. 86/05.
32. 'The Official Gazette of BiH', No. 15/06.
33. 'The Official Gazette of BiH', No. 15/06.
34. 'The Official Gazette of BiH', No. 15/06.

9. Regulation on Definition of a Dominant Position.[35]
10. Decision on Block Exemption Granted to Certain Categories of Vertical Agreements (between undertakings operating on different levels of production or distribution).[36]
11. Regulation on Block Exemption Granted to Agreements on Distribution and Servicing of Motor Vehicles.[37]
12. Decision on Notification and Criteria for the Assessment of a Concentration of Undertakings.
13. Regulation on Annexes and Amendments of the Regulation on Definition of Categories of Dominant Position.
14. Decision on Annexes and Amendments of the Regulation on the Definition of a Relevant Market.
15. Decision on Annexes and Amendments of the Regulation on Agreements of Minor Importance.
16. Decision on Notification and Criteria for the Assessment of a Concentration of Undertakings.
17. Decision on the Procedure for Granting Immunity from Fines (Leniency Policy).

II. Guidelines

40. The Council of Competition, pursuant to Article 25, paragraph 1, point a), in connection with Article 35, paragraph 1, point b) of the and Article 61, paragraph 2 of the Law on Administration,[38] at its 99th (ninety-ninth) session held on 17.02.2022, adopted the Instruction on the manner of data collection through direct inspection.

41. The Instruction, comprising eight articles, governs the manner of conducting data collection through the procedural act of direct inspection in proceedings initiated by a Conclusion to initiate proceedings before the Council of Competition, for the purpose of enabling the implementation of the LoC and the exercise of statutory powers.

42. The Instruction provides a definition of 'direct inspection' and prescribes the entities at which such inspection may be conducted and the conditions under which it may be carried out. It also designates the authorised officials who may perform the act of direct inspection.

43. Furthermore, the Instruction imposes an obligation on the Council of Competition to deliver to the undertaking a Request that must include:

– the legal basis;

---

35. 'The Official Gazette of BiH', No. 18/06.
36. 'The Official Gazette of BiH', No. 18/06.
37. 'The Official Gazette of BiH', No. 16/06.
38. 'The Official Gazette of BiH' Nos 32/02, 102/09, and 72/17,

- the subject matter and purpose of the request;
- the deadline for its execution; and
- a warning regarding the possibility of imposing sanctions for non-compliance, in accordance with Articles 49 and 51 of the LoC.

The Instruction also regulates the procedure for data collection itself, as well as issues concerning confidential business information.

§4. Sources' Relation and Hierarchy

44. The legal order of Bosnia and Herzegovina is systemised in line with the principle of hierarchy, so in the case of collision of legal norms, the norm of legal act of superior legal force is applied, and in the case of legal acts of the same force, the principles of *lex specialis derogat legi generali* and *lex posterior derogat legi priori* are applied.

I. The Law on Competition

45. The main goal of the Law on Competition of BiH is to establish a more efficient market competition protection mechanism in Bosnia and Herzegovina, to strengthen and set up a single market at the level of state, and to enable better cooperation between business entities and national body in charge of market competition protection. Sixty-two articles of this Law, systemised into four sections, regulate the rules, measures and the procedure of market competition protection, as well as the competences and the way the Council of Competition of BiH should operate to protect and promote the market competition in Bosnia and Herzegovina.[39]

§5. Role and Authority of Precedents

46. The legal system of Bosnia and Herzegovina belongs to the European continental law, in which the norms are codified into laws and by-laws.

47. In line with the 'harmonisation clause' and the provision of SAA contained in the Article 71, paragraph 2 of the SAA, which prescribes that any practices contrary to this Article shall be assessed on the basis of criteria arising from the application of the competition rules applicable in the EU and interpretative instruments adopted by the EU institutions, the European Commission and the European Court of Justice, the precedent practice was introduced in BiH.

39. *See*; Kanita Imamović-Čizmić, Market Competition Legal Protection Mechanism in Bosnia and Herzegovina, LAP LAMBERT Academic Publishing (20 May 2014) p. 56.

48. The provision of Article 43, paragraph 7 of the LoC specifies that, in favour of the assessment of the case in question, the Council of Competition may apply the practice of the European Court of Justice and the decisions of the European Commission.

49. The provision of the Article 71, paragraph 2 of the SAA, has set a higher standard in this because it demands mandatory assessment of the case before the national bodies in charge of protecting the competition law based on judicial practice of the European Court of Justice and the decisions of the European Commission to the extent in which it can have an impact on the trade between the EU and BiH.

50. The trials in BiH still rely on the interpretation of the law upon determining the state of facts, but the judicial practice of the European Court of Justice and the practice of the European Commission are taken as one of the rules of interpretation and assessment by analogy. Ultimately, if the decision of the domestic judiciary is based on analogy with some decision of the European Court of Justice, it will have the significance of a legal source for the solution of a specific case if its significance is of prevailing importance for the solution of a specific case.[40]

40. Branko Morait, Sloboda ugovaranja i pravo konkurencije u savremenoj sudskoj praksi, Pravna riječ, (36) Banja Luka, 2013, 101–117.

Chapter 2. Scope of Application

§1. Territorial Reach

51. Article 2 of the Law on Competition specifies its enforcement in a way that the 'Law applies to all natural and legal persons who are directly or indirectly engaged in the production, sale of goods and services, involved in trade of goods and services and who with their actions can prevent, restrict or distort competition in the entire territory of Bosnia and Herzegovina or significant part of the market.' This Law shall also apply to all economic activities of the undertakings that have their seat or permanent residence abroad, if their activities have substantial effect on the market of Bosnia and Herzegovina or its relevant parts.

§2. Special Sectors

52. In the market of Bosnia and Herzegovina, there are no sectors which are subject to special regulations on competition which deviate from the general provisions of the Law on Competition.

53. Observed as a whole, the market in Bosnia and Herzegovina is not fully liberalised and there are certain legal obstructions present in terms of accessing certain markets, and most of them stem from the legal conditions for acquiring the state licence or the licence to register business, such as law firms, doctors' offices and institutes and accounting services. However, certain sectors are still under the control of the state, or only the licensed business entities can compete in these markets.

§3. State-Owned Enterprises and Public Utilities

54. Traditionally, in Bosnia and Herzegovina, the energy and its distribution, telecommunications, public transportation and postal services are all sectors in which state-owned enterprises are predominant and are under state control.

55. The status of a potential EU membership candidate brings along many changes in the light of liberalisation of the sectors of energy, telecommunications and postal services in BiH and certain steps forward have been made in this direction.

I. Energy

56. In the energy market of Bosnia and Herzegovina, there are three producers, suppliers and distributors of electricity, which are traditionally owned by the state, meaning the entities, and there is also the Brcko District utility company. The Treaty on the Energy Community (ratified in 2000) specifies the creation of a legal framework for the establishment of free energy market, but its enforcement has been significantly decelerated, especially due to absence of transparent energy policies, insufficient investments in energy efficiency, and slow-paced modernisation of legislation.[41]

57. The SAA demands the adoption of European directives and standards relating to energy and Bosnia and Herzegovina has been placed before many demands that came as a result of its membership in the Energy Community of South East Europe.

58. Some progress towards the modernisation of the legal framework for the energy market in BiH has been made with the adoption of the law on electric power and the establishment of new (which did not exist before) institutions such as DERK (State Electricity Regulatory Commission), NOS (Independent System Operator) and Elektroprijenos (Company for the transmission of electric power in BiH) on state level, and FERK (Regulatory Commission for Energy in FBiH) and REERS (Regulatory Commission for Energy of RS).[42]

59. The process of liberalisation of this market began with the DERK Decision on Scope, Conditions and Time Schedule of Electricity Market Opening in Bosnia and Herzegovina.

II. Telecommunications

60. Since the dissolution of SFRY, and the subsequent division of the former SOUTHERN PTT of BiH into three operators, Bosnia and Herzegovina became the only country in the region to enter the liberalisation process with three state-owned operators.

61. At this moment, there are three dominant operators on the telecommunications market (fixed and mobile telephony) in Bosnia and Herzegovina. The specificity can be seen in the fact that certain operators act as monopolists in certain geographical regions with certain ethnic composition of the population.

62. The share of alternative operators in the market of fixed telephony is 4.43%, while the percentage in the market of mobile telephony in 2013 was only 0.53%. When it comes to the market of internet services in Bosnia and Herzegovina, it can be said that it is very competitive since there were seventy-five internet providers registered in 2012.[43]

---

41. 'BILTEN' GASBiH Februar 2012, br. 23, str.7.
42. Centar za politike i upravljanje, Izvještaj o politikama energetskog sektora u Bosni i Hercegovini Septembar 2010. str.2.
43. Boris Mandić, 'Problem oligopola na tržištu telekomunijskijskih usluga u BiH', Mastrer rad, Pravni fakultet Sarajevo, 2013. str.79.

63. BiH is one of the first regional countries to launch the liberalisation process as early as 2006, and the main role of the regulator was granted to the Regulatory Communications Agency of Bosnia and Herzegovina, which operates as an independent body.

III. Postal Services

64. The specificity of the postal services market in BiH is reflected in the fact that there are three public operators and eleven privately owned operators competing in it. The process of liberalisation of postal services in BiH has been launched. There is no special regulation of competition on this market.

§4. Sensible Effect and De Minimis

65. Article 8 of the LoC regulates the institute of agreements of minor importance. According to this Article, the prohibition in Article 4 paragraph (1) of the Law on Competition is not applied to agreements of minor importance. According to the Law on Competition, *agreement of minor importance* is an agreement when the joint market share of the parties to the agreement and economic entities under their control in the relevant market is insignificant, except for the severe constraints.

66. In order for an agreement to be exempted under the *de minimis rule*, in line with Article 8 paragraph 3 of the LoC, one of the following conditions has to be met:

a. when the total market share of participants in the agreement in the relevant market does not exceed 10%, in a case when the agreement is concluded between economic entities that are actual or potential competitors, that is, they operate on the same level of production or trade;
b. where the market share of each party in the relevant market does not exceed 15%, in a case when the economic agreement is concluded between economic entities which are not actual or potential competitors, that is, they operate at different levels of production or trade;
c. in agreements where it is difficult to determine whether they are concluded between competition or economic entities that are not competitors, the threshold of 10% will be applied.

In 2005, the Council of Competition adopted the Regulation on Agreements of Minor Importance and more closely defined the conditions and criteria that the agreements of minor importance have to meet, and also regulated the possibility of a parallel network of agreements, as well as severe constraints.

67. The Article 4 of the Regulation specifies that in cases where competition in the relevant market is restricted or infringed by the cumulative effect of agreements on the sale of products or services concluded between different suppliers or distributors, that is to say, in cases where parallel networks of agreements have similar effects on the market, the insignificant share of each of the parties to the agreement or their controlled undertakings will be deemed a market share of up to 5%, for agreements concluded between competing undertakings and for agreements concluded between non-competing undertakings. If the relevant market is covered by parallel network of agreements whose market share is less than 30%, it means that the cumulative effect of a parallel network of agreements does not restrict or distort market competition.

68. Articles 7 and 8 of the Regulation on Agreements of Minor Importance regulate hardcore restrictions to horizontal agreements which have the characteristics of an agreement of minor importance if they aim to:

a. fix prices when selling the products to third parties;
b. limit output or sales;
c. allocate markets or customers;

and for vertical agreements if they aim to:

a. limit a buyer's ability to determine its sale price, irrespective of the supplier's possibility to impose a maximum sale price or recommend a sale price, provided that the prices do not amount to a fixed or minimum sale price that is a result of pressure from, or incentives offered by, any of the parties;
b. restrict the territory where the buyer may sell products from the agreement, or restrict the sale of contracted products to a certain group of consumers, except for the following cases:
   - active sales on the exclusively allocated territory or to an exclusive customer group reserved for the supplier or allocated by the supplier to another buyer, provided that such a restriction does not disable further sales of the product by an indirect buyer;
   - sales to end users by a buyer operating at the wholesale level of trade;
   - sales to unauthorised distributors imposed by the members of a selective distribution system;
   - possibility of a buyer to sell components, supplied for the purposes of embedding, to other customers who would use them to manufacture the same type of products as those produced by the supplier.
c. restrict active or passive selling to end users by members of a selective distribution network operating at the retail level of trade, not excluding the possibility of prohibition to a member of the distribution network from selling using unauthorised undertaking;
d. restrict mutual supply of products between distributors within a selective distribution system, including the distributions between distributors operating at different levels of trade;

e. restrict, by agreement between a supplier of components and a buyer who incorporates those components, the supplier's ability to sell the components as spare parts to end users or to independent repairers or other service providers not entrusted by the buyer with the repair or servicing of its products.

Chapter 3. Overview of Substantive Provisions

§1. Restrictive Agreements

69. Article 4 paragraph 1 of the Law on Competition specifies as prohibited all agreements, contracts, single provision of agreements or contracts, concerted practices, explicit and tacit agreements between the undertakings, as well as decisions by associations of undertakings the object or effect of which is to prevent, restrict or distort market competition in the relevant market, and in particular those which: (a) directly or indirectly fix purchase and selling prices or any other trading conditions; (b) limit or control the production, markets, technical development or investment; (c) share markets or sources of supply; (d) apply dissimilar conditions to equivalent transactions with other undertakings, thereby placing them at a competitive disadvantage; (e) make the conclusion of contracts subject to acceptance by the other parties of supplementary obligations which, by their nature or according to commercial usage, have no connection with the subject of such contracts.

70. Paragraph 2 of Article 4 of the Law on Competition declares that any agreements prohibited pursuant to paragraph 1 of this Article are null and void. On 27 May 2015, the Council of Competition reached a Decision which determined that the Government of the FBiH, with the Article VII of the special criteria of the Decision on the list of essential medicine necessary to ensure healthcare protection within the standards of mandatory health insurance in FBiH, prevents, restricts and distorts the market competition in the market of prescribed medicines which are issued at the expense of cantonal health insurance institutes in the FBiH, by restricting and controlling the market, which represents prohibited agreement in the sense of Article 4, paragraph (1), item (b) of the Law on Competition.[44]

I. Exemptions

71. Paragraph 3 of Article 4 of the Law on Competition defines the general rule of exemption and specifies that agreements in terms of paragraph 1 of Article 4 are not prohibited if they contribute to improving the production or distribution of goods and/or services within Bosnia and Herzegovina or if they contribute the promotion of technical or economic progress, while allowing consumers a fair share of the resulting benefit, and which:

a. impose only restrictions necessary to the achievement of these objectives;

44. In the same Decision, the Council of Competition has concluded that the said provisions of the Decision on the list of essential medicines necessary to ensure healthcare protection within the standards of mandatory health insurance in the Federation of Bosnia and Herzegovina are null and void (*ex lege*), and ordered the Government of the Federation of Bosnia and Herzegovina to immediately, and in the period of no more than thirty days, harmonise the provisions of the Decision. For the violation of the Law on Competition, the Council of Competition has sanctioned the Government of the Federation of Bosnia and Herzegovina with a fine of BAM 80,000.

b. do not enable the elimination of competition in the substantial part of products or services in question. While performing the proceedings in question, the Council of Competition has applied the provisions of the Law on Competition, Regulation on Block Exemption of Agreements Between Undertakings Operating on Different Levels of Production or Distribution Chain (vertical agreements) ('The Official Gazette of BiH', No. 18/06), Regulation on Block Exemption Granted to Agreements on the Transfer of Technology, Licence and Know-how Agreements ('The Official Gazette of BiH', No. 15/06) and the Regulation on the Definition of a Relevant Market ('The Official Gazette of BiH', Nos 18/06 and 34/10). The justification of the decision reads that when assessing the agreements in question, the Council of Competition took into account the clarification of the Applicant that they will improve the production and distribution of goods and services in Bosnia and Herzegovina, which reads as follows: – advantages in terms of prices – introduction of modern technologies in the production process. The Council of Competition took a stance that the Applicant has sufficiently argued for the case and proved that the conditions prescribed by Law for individual exemption of the concerned restrictive Agreement have been met, since the Agreement in question will contribute to the improvement of production and distribution of goods and/or services in Bosnia and Herzegovina, promotion of technical and economic development, whereby it will enable the consumers to enjoy a fair share of benefits stemming from it because the conclusion and implementation of the concerned Agreement only impose the restrictions necessary to achieve the goals and do not exclude the competition in the significant part of concerned products and/or services, pursuant to Article 4, paragraph (3) of the Law.[45]

The Article 5 of the Law on Competition regulates the registration procedure for individual exemptions according to which the Council of Competition can, at the request of one or more of the parties to the agreement, make a decision on granting an individual exemption from the application of the agreement prohibition referred to in Article 4, paragraph (1) of the Law on Competition, if that particular agreement fulfils the general rules on exemption in the sense of the Law. The solution on exemption also determines the time limit of exemptions which, according to Article 6 of the Law on Competition – cannot be longer than five years and can be additionally extended only once for no more than five years.

72. The Law on Competition has imposed an obligation on the Council of Competition to adopt special acts which would enable block exemptions from the enforcement of Article 4, paragraph 3 of the Law, and in particular:

45. On 10 Sep. 2015, the Council of Competition of Bosnia and Herzegovina has adopted a Decision Number: 04-26-4-39-18-II/14 which determines individual exemption of the Agreement on the regulation of competition between the undertaking Jaegersberger GmbH Pernitz, Austria as the buyer and the undertaking ĆOSIĆPROMEX d.o.o., Usora, BiH and natural person Mijo Cosic (…)** as the buyer, pursuant to Art. 4, paras (1) and (3) and Art. 5 of the Law on Competition. Individual exemption is determined for the time period of five years.

a. horizontal agreements, in particular the agreements on research and development and specialisation;
b. vertical agreements, in particular the agreements on exclusive distribution, selective distribution, exclusive purchase and franchising;
c. agreements on transfer of technology, licence and know-how agreements;
d. agreements on distribution and servicing of motor vehicles;
e. insurance agreements.

73. In line with that, the Council of Competition has so far adopted: Regulation on Block Exemption Between Undertakings Operating on the Same Level of Production or Distribution Chain (horizontal agreements) Relating Particularly to Research, Development and Specialisation Agreements; Regulation on Block Exemption Granted to Agreements on the Transfer of Technology, Licence and Know-how Agreements; Regulation on Block Exemption Granted to Insurance Agreements; Regulation on Definition of Categories of Dominant Position; Regulation on Block Exemption of Agreements Between Undertakings Operating on Different Levels of Production or Distribution Chain (vertical agreements); Regulation on Block Exemption Granted to Agreements on Distribution and Servicing of Motor Vehicles.

§2. Dominant Undertakings

74. In line with the paragraph 1 of Article 9 of the Law on Competition, an undertaking has a dominant position in the relevant market of goods or services, when due to its market power it can act in the relevant market considerably independently of its actual or potential competitors, buyers, consumers or suppliers, taking into account the market share of that undertaking in the relevant market, market shares of its competitors in that market, as well as the legal and other barriers to the entry of other undertakings in the market.[46]

75. Paragraphs 2, 3, 4 of Article 9 of the Law on Competition answer the question of how large portion of the market share an undertaking or several of them can hold until they can be presumed to be in a dominant position. It assumes that an undertaking is dominant in the relevant market of products and services where it holds a market share exceeding 40%. An undertaking may be dominant if it holds a market share of less than 40% if other indicators (e.g., bad position and small market share of the existing competitors, serious barriers to entering the relevant market for other undertakings) prove its dominant position. It assumes that two or more undertakings may be dominant in the relevant market of products and services if their market share jointly accounts for more than 60%. It assumes that four or more

46. In the case of M.R.M. export-import d.o.o. for trade, marketing and services from Ljubuski, against Asa Auto d.o.o. Sarajevo, the Council of Competition has determined that 'Asa Auto has a dominant position on the market of Volkswagen vehicle sales, given the fact that thanks to the exclusive agreements with the Volkswagen Group AG (Federal Republic of Germany), it became the only authorised importer of products from the Volkswagen brand in the territory of BiH.'

undertakings may be dominant in the relevant market of products and services if their market share jointly accounts for more than 80%.

76. Article 10 of the Law on Competition prescribes the specific conditions under which certain activities of the undertakings which have a dominant position are considered abuse of that position, and the phrase 'particularly if this activity relates to' carries the list of examples.

77. Pursuant to Article 10 of the Law on Competition, abuse of dominant position exists in cases where one or more undertakings which have a dominant position are responsible for the following:

a. direct or indirect imposition of unfair purchase or selling prices or other trading conditions which restrict competition;
b. limitation of production, markets or technical development to the prejudice of consumers;
c. application of dissimilar conditions to equivalent or similar transactions with other parties, thereby placing them at a competitive disadvantage;
d. making the conclusion of the contracts subject to acceptance by the other party of supplementary obligations which, by their nature or according to commercial usage, have no connection with subject matter of such contract.[47]

In 2006, the Council of Competition adopted the Regulation on the Definition of Categories of Dominant Position, in which it specified the categories, conditions and methods for determining the dominant position of an undertaking and the criteria of abuse of the dominant position.

Pursuant to Article 3, paragraph 1 of the Regulation on the Definition of Categories of Dominant Position, undertakings do not have the dominant position unless they have significant market force in the relevant market in relation to the actual or potential competitors, and especially in relation to the following criteria:

a. market share (the volume of sale and purchase in the relevant market of products or services; financial strength or production capacities);
b. structures of the relevant market and the economic relation with the competition;
c. ability to maintain the prices above the level of competitiveness (restricts production and quality);
d. access to sources of procurement (raw materials) or the distribution channels;

47. On 20 Nov. 2013, the Council of Competition of Bosnia and Herzegovina has reached a Decision which determined that the undertaking Apatinska pivara Apatin d.o.o., (Republic of Serbia), refusing to sign the Sale-Purchase Agreement for the year 2012 with the undertaking Preduzece za spoljnu i unutrasnju trgovinu i usluge Dejan komerc d.o.o., BiH, abused its dominant market position in the distribution and sale of beer in the territory of the Republic of Srpska, pursuant to Art. 10, para. (2), item c) of the Law on Competition for which the Council has imposed a fine on the undertaking Apatinska pivara d.o.o. Apatin, in the amount of BAM 430,000 and ordered Apatinska pivara Apatin d.o.o. to sign the Sale-Purchase Agreement under the same conditions with Preduzece za spoljnu i unutrasnju trgovinu i usluge Dejan komerc d.o.o.

e. levels of vertical integration of the relevant market;
f. economic regulators, investment obstacles to entry/exit of potential undertakings in the relevant market;
g. technological advantages, patents, intellectual and industrial ownership rights and similar rights.

§3. Concentrations

78. Pursuant to Article 12 of the Law on Competition, a concentration is defined as:

a. joining or merger of two or more previously independent undertakings or parts of undertakings;
b. the acquisition of control or prevailing influence of one or more undertakings over another undertaking, or over more undertakings or a part of another undertaking, or the parts of another undertaking, in particular by:
   1. acquisition of the majority of shares or share capital by means of purchase;[48] or
   2. acquisition of the majority of voting rights; or
   3. some other way, pursuant to the provisions of this Law, which regulate the establishment of economic subjects and their management.
c. the creation of a joint venture, by two or more independent undertakings, on a lasting basis.

79. Article 12 of the Law on Competition specifies the ways in which it is possible to acquire control over undertakings by holding rights, contracts or any means by which one or more undertakings, either solely or jointly, within the specific legal and factual circumstances, are enabled the possibility to exercise predominant influence over one or more undertakings.

80. Paragraph 3 of Article 12 of the Law on Competition specifies the condition under which the acquisition of control by banks and financial institutions over an undertaking in their ordinary activities of business is not considered a concentration. This paragraph specifies that the acquisition of control over an undertaking by persons that perform the function of bankruptcy and liquidation administrator in the

48. The Council of Competition has reached a Decision (number: 02-26-1-06-13-II/12 of 7 Aug. 2012) which assessed as allowed the concentration on the market of production and distribution of milk and dairy products in the territory of Bosnia and Herzegovina which arose from control acquisition of the undertaking Akcionarsko drustvo industrija mleka i mlecnih proizvoda 'Imlek', (Republic of Serbia), and the undertaking Društvo sa ogranicenom odgovornoscu za proizvodnju 'Mlijeko-produkt' Kozarska Dubica over the undertaking Društvo sa ogranicenom odgovornoscu za proizvodnju i usluge 'NATURA-MILK' Bosnia and Herzegovina, through purchase of 100% ownership share by the undertaking Drustvo sa ogranicenom odgovornoscu za proizvodnju i usluge 'NATURA-VITA' Blatnica-Teslic, BiH.

sense of the law on bankruptcy and liquidation is not considered a concentration, and also lays down the conditions according to which a joint venture between more undertakings is not considered a concentration but is assessed in relation to the institute of prohibited agreements.

81. Article 13 of the Law on Competition defines the prohibited concentrations of undertakings that significantly impede effective market competition, in the whole territory of Bosnia and Herzegovina or in a relevant part of it, and particularly, that create a new or strengthen an existing dominant position.

§4. Other Prohibitions

82. The Law on the Competition does not specify other prohibitions in the sense of suspension of state aid to economic entities allocated from the public funds for the support of certain forms of trade.

§5. Tests of Illegality

83. Tests of legality of certain activities in the sense of provisions of the Law on Competition exist in the competition law of BiH.

I. Per Se Prohibitions and Naked Restraints

84. In order for the prohibition of certain activities in line with the Law on Competition to exist, certain conditions have to be met. There is a dilemma whether the 'per se' rule in the spirit of the Sherman Act, which prohibits 'any agreement or contract which restricts the trade and business between the federal states', is incorporated in the competition law of Bosnia and Herzegovina. If we analyse the Article 4 of the Law on Competition, it can be said that the paragraph 1 of this Article contains a 'looser' form of prohibition 'per se' because it prescribes that the prohibited agreements are those which: (a) directly or indirectly fix purchase and selling prices or any other trading conditions; (b) limit or control the production, markets, technical development or investment; (c) share markets or sources of supply; (d) apply dissimilar conditions to equivalent transactions with other undertakings, thereby placing them at a competitive disadvantage; (e) make the conclusion of contracts subject to acceptance by the other parties of supplementary obligations which, by their nature or according to commercial usage, have no connection with the subject of such contracts. The 'per se' rule is applied in Article 11, paragraph 1 of the Law on Competition, which 'prohibits any abuse of the dominant position of one or more undertakings in the relevant market' and which does not stipulate any exemptions from the application.

II. Balancing Tests

85. A looser form of the 'per se' rule exists because of the application of the 'rule of reason' test where, pursuant to paragraph 3 of Article 4 of the Law on Competition, which represents exemptions from the application of the prohibitions, it is assessed whether the effects of the agreement exceed what can be called justified, reasonable and appropriate restriction and disruption of the competition.

III. Merger Tests

86. The Law on Competition has fully incorporated the SIEC test in the provisions of Article 13, prescribing that there 'shall be prohibited the concentrations of undertakings that significantly impede effective market competition, in the whole territory of Bosnia and Herzegovina or in a relevant part of it, and particularly, that create a new or strengthen an existing dominant position'.

87. Article 17 of the Law on Competition (Appraisal of intended concentration) specifies that in making the assessment of intended concentration, the Council of Competition will analyse the effects which could result in the significant distortion of market competition, or whether that concentration creates or strengthens dominant position, in particular: (a) the structure of the relevant market; (b) the effects of the concentration concerned on other actual and potential competitors; (c) the market position of parties in competition, their market shares, economic and financial power; (d) alternatives available to suppliers and users; (e) economic, legal and other barriers to entry to the market; (f) level of internal and international competitiveness of the parties to concentration; (g) supply and demand trends for the relevant goods and/or services; (h) the trends of technical and economic progress; (i) consumers′ interests.

88. Article 17 (Criteria for the Assessment of Concentration) of the Decision on the Notification and Criteria for the Assessment of a Concentration in Undertakings specifies that in the course of the assessment of the intended concentration, the Council of Competition will primarily analyse the effects which could result in significant distortion of the market competition.

Chapter 4. Overview of Main Notions

§1. Undertaking

89. Analogue to comparative law and practice, the concept of 'undertakings' in BiH represents the basis for main prohibitions of the Law on Competition in terms of restrictive agreements and the abuse of dominant position.

90. Article 2 of the Law on Competition, which defines the scope of application, also determines what is considered to be the meaning of the term undertakings. The provision in the paragraph 1 provides a general definition according to which the law is applied to all legal and natural persons who, directly or indirectly, participate in production, trade of goods or services and who, through their actions, prevent, restrict or distort market competition on the whole territory of Bosnia and Herzegovina or its relevant part, hereinafter called the undertakings. This provision is followed by the term 'particularly to', and it clarifies to which undertakings this refers to:

a. economic associations, enterprises, entrepreneurs, disregarding their form of property, seat or place of residence;
b. state and local self-government units directly or indirectly participating in or having influence on the market;
c. other natural or legal persons such as associations, sports organisations, institutions, cooperatives, intellectual property right holders, etc., that participate, indirectly or directly, permanently, temporary or single in the market, disregarding their legal status, form of property, seat or place of residence.

91. Paragraph 2 of Article 2 of the Law on Competition underlines that this Law will apply to connected undertakings, meaning an undertaking controlling another undertaking, and specifies the examples of control of the undertaking.

§2. Relevant Market

92. The relevant market is defined by Article 3 of the Law on Competition and regulated in detail by the Council of Competition Decision on the Definition of a Relevant Market. Article 3 of the Law on Competition also determines the geographic and production dimension of the market. In line with that, the geographic dimension is specified by paragraph 1, which states that the relevant market is 'defined as a market of certain products, which are the subject of the business operations performed by the undertakings in the specific geographic territory'. Paragraph 3 of the same Article more precisely determines the geographic dimension of the relevant market as a part or the whole geographic territory of BiH, where the undertakings operate in selling and/or purchasing of a relevant product under equal or sufficiently homogeneous conditions and which are significantly distinguished from the conditions of competition in neighbouring geographic markets.[49] Also, paragraph 4 of Article 3 of the Law on Competition, which was later incorporated in the Decision of the Council of Competition, stipulates the possibility that 'in specific cases, a relevant geographic market may be defined on the international level'.

93. Paragraph 2 of Article 3 of the Law on Competition recognises the production dimension of the relevant market by specifying that 'a relevant product market comprises all products which consumers and/or users consider mutually substitutable, under acceptable conditions, having in mind the products' characteristics, their quality, intended use, way of usage and the price and sale conditions'.

94. The Council of Competition Decision on the Definition of a Relevant Market of 2006 separates the definitions of geographic and production markets, which are calculated individually by taking into account the criteria provided by Article 6 of the Decision:

a. demand substitutability for the particular product;
b. supply substitutability for the particular product;
c. existence of potential market competition;
d. barriers to entry to the relevant market.

95. Pursuant to Article 7 of the Decision on the Definition of a Relevant Market, the assessment of demand substitutability of specific product refers to the determination of products which are viewed by customers as mutually substitutable, whereby the following criteria are taken into account: the time period that suppliers need to adjust to normal supplying of market with a substitute product (substitute), the prevailing market price of the particular product if the price is determined in absence of effective competition, and those consumers (buyers) who are not able, despite of the change in the price of relevant product, to accept the substitute product (substitute).

96. In line with the Decision on the Definition of a Relevant Market, the demand substitutability is based on the presumption that a certain product is substitutable (substitute), which can be foreseen logically when a significant number of consumers (buyers) of the relevant product switch to another product, or to another supplier of the equal (similar) product, in response to a hypothetically small, in the range of 5% to 10%, but permanent price increase of the relevant product.

---

49. In its practice so far, the Council of Competition has determined as a relevant geographic market the market of the whole Bosnia and Herzegovina, as the biggest one, markets of entities, cantons and municipalities, as well as the smallest ones possible such as the bus station in the case of Centrotrans Eurolines d.d. (Decision of the Council of Competition of Bosnia and Herzegovina Number 01-01-26-007-13-II/08 of 12 Jun. 2008).

97. In line with Article 9 of the Decision on the Definition of a Relevant Market, the supply substitutability for a certain product means the ability of the producer (distributor) to, in the case of increase in price of the relevant product, switch to production or distribution of a substitute product in a short time, without incurring significant additional costs or risks.

98. When estimating the existence of potential market competition, it is necessary to determine its level and conditions in the relevant market under which the new market participants, that is, the undertakings, may enter the relevant market.

99. Pursuant to Article 10 of the Decision on the Definition of a Relevant Market, the existence of potential market competition is determined on the basis of foreseeable changes of the existing market condition, particularly taking into account the following criteria:

a. structure of relevant market;
b. behaviour of existing participants in a relevant market and influence on other actual and potential market participants;
c. economic and financial powers of the market participants and their ability to choose suppliers and users;
d. economic, legal and other barriers to entry to a relevant market;
e. trends in the market in respect of supply, demand, economic and technical development of a relevant product;
f. the market share indicators among market participants (national and international);
g. analysis of price changes and price discrepancies at national and international levels.

Article 11, paragraph 1 of the Decision on the Definition of a Relevant Market lays down the general definition of the barriers to entry to a relevant market in the sense of all obstacles which limit and restrict free access to the market to potential market participants (undertakings).

Paragraph 2 of Article 11 of the Decision on the Definition of a Relevant Market specifies what can be considered as particular obstacles to entry to a relevant market:

a. legal barriers, law regulations, by-law acts and administrative regulations (e.g., duty and other import taxes, quantitative and value restrictions, policy on taxes and prices, state monopoly, technical regulations, norms and standards and likewise);
b. economic barriers, especially:
   1. structural barriers (initial capital, capital investments, patents, know-how, economy of scale, transportation costs, differentiation of products, supply and demand level and similar barriers);
   2. strategic barriers for access to a relevant market created by the existing participants, whose behaviour and activities preclude and prevent other potential market participants from entering the relevant market.

The Decision on the Definition of a Relevant Market provides guidelines for the definition of a relevant market in specific cases.

§3. Market Power/Dominant Position

100. The institute of dominant position in the competition law in Bosnia and Herzegovina is defined by the Law on Competition and more precisely regulated by the Council of Competition Decision on the Definition of Dominant Position of 2006.

101. Article 9 of the Law on Competition provides a clearer definition and specifies the conditions for the existence of dominant position by prescribing that 'an undertaking has a dominant position in the relevant market of goods or services, when due to its market power it can act in the relevant market considerably independently of its actual or potential competitors, buyers, consumers or suppliers, taking into account the market share of that undertaking in the relevant market, market shares of its competitors in that market, as well as the legal and other barriers to the entry of other undertakings in the market'.

102. Paragraph 2 of the Law uses the formulation that 'an undertaking will be presumed to be in a dominant position in the market of goods and services, if it holds more than 40% of the market share in the relevant market'.

103. In terms of situations involving more undertakings, paragraph 3 of the Law uses the formulation that 'more undertakings will be presumed to be in a dominant position in the market of goods and/or services, if the joint market share of two or more undertakings in the relevant market exceeds 60%'.

104. The formulation in paragraph 4 specifies that 'more undertakings will be presumed to be in a dominant position in the market of goods and/or services, if the joint market share of four or five undertakings in the relevant market exceeds 80%'.

105. The use of terminology 'will be presumed to be' implies that the definition of a dominant position specified in the Article 9 of the Law on Competition follows the definition from the United Brands judgment, so it will be presumed that an undertaking has a dominant position in the relevant market of goods or services, when due to its market power it can act in the relevant market considerably independently of its actual or potential competitors, buyers, consumers or suppliers, and especially if it has no significant competitors in the relevant market, and/or if it has significant market strength in the relevant market in relation to actual or potential competitors.

106. Therefore, the Law on Competition (Article 9, paragraphs 2, 3 and 4), similar to the EU law, contains the presumption of presence of a dominant position of two or more undertakings whose market share in the relevant market exceeds 40%, 60% and 80%.

107. Articles 2 and 3 of the Decision on the Definition of Categories of Dominant Position specify that an undertaking has a dominant position in the relevant market of products or services.

108. Pursuant to Article 2 of the Decision on the Definition of Categories of Dominant Position, there are two criteria for the existence of dominant position:

1. when, due to its market power, an undertaking can behave and operate largely independent of actual or potential competitors, buyers, consumers or suppliers, and thus restricts or prevents efficient competition;
2. if there is no competition or if existing competition is insignificant.

It can be concluded from the above-stated that the main condition for the existence of a dominant position is market power, meaning that an undertaking does not have a dominant position in the relevant market of products or services unless it has significant market power.

In line with Article 3 of the Decision on Definition of Categories of Dominant Position, an undertaking does not have a dominant position in the relevant market of products and services if its market power is not significant. An undertaking has significant market power in the relevant market in relation to actual or potential competitors, particularly regarding the following criteria:

a. market share (scale of sale and purchase in the relevant market of products or services; financial power or production capacities);
b. structure of the relevant market and economic relations with competitors;
c. ability to maintain the prices above the competition level (restricts production and quality);
d. access to supply sources (raw materials) or distribution channels;
e. vertical integration levels of the relevant market;
f. economic regulators, investment obstacles for potential undertakings to enter/exit the relevant market;
g. technological advantages, patents, intellectual or industrial property rights and similar rights.

According to Article 14 of the Decision on the Definition of Categories of Dominant Position, market share of an undertaking operating in the relevant market is calculated based on the market share of production and/or sale of a relevant product in the relevant market during certain period of time. Market share is the measure of appropriate size of every undertaking in the relevant market. The said market share is calculated based on total value and the volume of production and/or trade (according to the total amount of appropriate units of measure and value) of the relevant product. An additional criterion is the use of data on production capacity of an undertaking in relation to total capacities that are used in production of a relevant product. In order to determine the estimated market share of a participant on the market, meaning an undertaking, other indicators (quantity and market value of the reserves of natural resources which the undertaking owns, controls and similar) are used as well. The time limit for specifying the market share is determined annually, and if it is necessary, it can also be determined for a longer or shorter period (monthly, quarterly), depending on the product and data which is collected, but the total time period for which the data on market share is collected cannot be longer than five years. The selection of the method, meaning the criteria for determining the market share for every given case will depend on the availability, accuracy and credibility of the existing data. Article 15 of the Decision lays down what is considered to be a relevant source of information for calculating the share, for example: data and information of undertakings-parties to the procedure and other, different professional associations of undertakings, statistics agencies, CBBiH, banking agencies, competent ministries and other public administration bodies, different regulatory agencies, independent market research agencies, units of local self-governance and the data of the Council of Competition.

§4. Agreements and Concerted Practices

109. Paragraph 1 of Article 4 of the Law on Competition lays down the definition of prohibited agreements, which reads that:

> there will be prohibited all agreements, contracts, single provision of agreements or contracts, concerted practices, explicit and tacit agreements between the undertakings, as well as decisions by associations of undertakings the object or effect of which is to prevent, restrict or distort market competition in the relevant market, and in particular those which:
>
> a. directly or indirectly fix purchase and selling prices or any other trading conditions;
> b. limit or control the production, markets, technical development or investment;
> c. share markets or sources of supply;
> d. apply dissimilar conditions to equivalent transactions with other undertakings, thereby placing them at a competitive disadvantage;
> e. make the conclusion of contracts subject to acceptance by the other parties of supplementary obligations which, by their nature or according to commercial usage, have no connection with the subject of such contracts.

According to this definition, agreements include: agreements, contracts, single provisions of agreements or contracts, concerted practices, explicit and tacit agreements between the undertakings, as well as decisions by associations of undertakings.

110. Agreements are: contracts, explicit and tacit agreements, concerted practices and decisions by associations of undertakings.

111. Such agreements are *ex lege* void if they cannot be exempted in a group or individually.

112. Article 43, paragraph 7 of the Law on Competition specifies that, in favour of the assessment of the case in question, the Council of Competition may apply the practice of the European Court of Justice and the decisions of the European Commission. If we add to this the commitment under Article 71, paragraph 2 of the SAA between the European Communities and their Member States and BiH, which specifies that any practices contrary to this Article (this refers to Article 71, paragraph 1 which prohibits anti-competition activities) will be assessed on the basis of criteria arising from the application of the competition rules applicable in the Community, in particular from Articles 101, 102, 106 and 107 of the Treaty on the Functioning of the EU and interpretative instruments adopted by the Community institutions, it is clear that the Council of Competition has plenty of instruments to assess the competition.

113. To prove the presence of 'an agreement' between undertakings, especially in cases where there is no material evidence (e.g., the signing of certain agreements, letters and other acts of correspondence between undertakings), represents an extremely difficult task which lies before the Council of Competition.

114. In the said cases, the presence of their coordinated activities in terms of increase or decrease of prices, interest rates or payment terms, content of instructions to organisational units of undertakings to which the suspicion of anti-competition activities relates to was taken as evidence.

115. The final assessment of the presence of agreement is provided after it has been determined that the condition or the effect on the market is a result of sound economic thinking and adjustment of undertakings to the changes in the market. Namely, once it has been established that there is a form of coordinated actions of the undertakings, certain precautions are necessary when automatically categorising such actions as agreed practices. Even though the coordinated actions might be an indicator that undertakings are in collusion, it would be premature to conclude the existence of agreed practices, due to the fact that the coordinated actions can appear through natural activities of oligopoly on the market. In such circumstances, proving the case can be very difficult. It is normal for competitors to adapt their activities to the conditions in the market and such adaptations are not always a result of conscious joint actions and coordinated activities. The process of proving the agreed practice needs to go towards proving the fact that the said coordinated actions on the market would not have taken place if there had not been contact between undertakings. It can be suspected that there is some form of secret agreement in place, because the signals from the market imply parallel price increases and similar activities. In such cases, the Council of Competition needs to prove the presence of an agreed practice before it makes a decision against certain companies.

116. In order to prove the presence of agreements, the Council of Competition has adopted the whistle-blower programme and adopted the Decision on the Procedure for Granting Immunity from Fines (Leniency Policy) in Sarajevo, in March

2010. The Decision defines the procedure for granting immunity or reducing the fines in cases when an undertaking participates in cartels, as well as conditions for granting immunity or reducing the fines.

§5. Restriction of Competition

117. Even though it appears at first that the institute of prohibited agreements is harmonised with the legal *acquis* of the EU, there are still some large discrepancies with significant consequences when enforcing the law in practice. Namely, unlike the provisions of Article 101 of the Treaty on the Functioning of the EU, Article 4 of the Law defines that in order for the agreements to be prohibited, their object or effect must be to prevent, restrict or distort competition. Also, besides that condition, they, in line with the same regulation, which is yet again different from the provision of Article 101 of the Treaty on the Functioning of the EU, must be ranked in one of the four types of agreements listed in paragraph 1 of Article 4 of the Law on Competition.

118. As a reminder, Article 101 of the Treaty on the Functioning of the EU defined the alternative conditions for the existence of the prohibition of agreements, which 'have as their object or effect the prevention, restriction or distortion of market competition on the relevant market' and provided an open list of examples of such agreements. Therefore, all agreements that meet the conditions of the general prohibition defined by paragraph 1 of Article 101 of the Treaty on the Functioning of the EU, from which the mentioned influence on the competition in internal market is set alternatively, are prohibited by the force of the law regardless of whether they are part of one of the groups in the so-called open list. It is clear that it is much harder to prove that both the object and consequence of distortion, restriction and prevention of competition exist. Even if it is proven that this condition exists, and the agreement does not fall under the listed agreements, it is exempted from the prohibition measures.

§6. Monopolisation and Abuse of Dominance

119. The second basic prohibition of anti-competition actions in the Law on Competition refers to the abuse of dominant position, which is regulated under Article 10 and can be considered harmonised with Article 102 of the Treaty on the Functioning of the EU.

120. General rule of prohibition or general prohibition was defined by paragraph 1 of Article 10 of the Law on competition in the following way: 'it is underlined that any abuse of dominant position by one or more undertakings in the relevant market is prohibited'.

121. Paragraph 2 of the same Article carries the list of potential actions of undertakings with dominant position which are considered by the force of law as abuses and are therefore prohibited:

a. direct or indirect imposition of unfair purchase or selling prices or other trading conditions which restrict competition;
b. limitation of production, markets or technical development to the prejudice of consumers;
c. application of dissimilar conditions to equivalent or similar transactions with other parties, thereby placing them at a competitive disadvantage;
d. making the conclusion of the contracts subject to acceptance by the other party of supplementary obligations which, by their nature or according to commercial usage, have no connection with subject matter of such contract.

§7. CONCENTRATIONS

122. Concentrations of undertakings, as a way of consolidation of capital or overcoming crises, the so-called crisis concentrations, are very often a matter to be decided by national bodies in charge of protecting market competition in countries in transition and development, such as BiH. They are less 'dangerous' to the market competition in relation to prohibited agreements and abuse of a dominant position. They are regulated by the Law on Competition and the by-law of the Council of Competition. The Law on Competition defines concentrations and prohibited concentrations, determines the total income for the control of concentration, mandatory notification and the procedure of passing the decision on the permissibility of concentration.

123. In 2010, the Council of Competition has also reached the Decision on Notification and Criteria for the Assessment of a Concentration of Undertakings, which regulates in detail the notifications of intended concentration of undertakings, the method of submission, the contents and form of the notification, the documentation and data which are to be enclosed to the notification, the form and contents of the announcement on acquisition of shares or share capital of the undertakings and the assessment criteria of the compatibility of concentrations of undertakings in the proceedings carried out by the Council of Competition within the meaning of the provisions stipulated by the Law on Competition. More on concentrations in Chapter 3. Overview of Substantive Provisions.

§8. JOINT VENTURES

124. Joint venture is regulated under Article 12, paragraph 1, item c), which defines that the creation of a joint venture, by two or more independent undertakings, on a lasting basis, is also considered a concentration. However, when a joint venture is aimed at coordinating market activities between two or more undertakings which remain independent, then this joint venture is not considered to be a concentration and will be assessed in line with Article (4) of the Law, meaning that it will be assessed whether the said situation is prohibited under Article 4.

Chapter 5. Consequences of Violations and Enforcement Institutions

§1. Administrative Enforcement

125. The general determinants of the existing mechanism for the enforcement of competition law in Bosnia and Herzegovina are a reflection of the overall socio-economic and political situation in which Bosnia and Herzegovina is right now.

126. For nearly half a century, Bosnia and Herzegovina has nurtured the concept of command economy in which competition was not perceived in the way it is perceived in modern market economies. Following the economic transition at the end of the last century and the dissolution of SFRY, a new stage in the development of competition law and policy in Bosnia and Herzegovina was launched. The mechanism for the enforcement of competition law in Bosnia and Herzegovina is a confirmation that, besides the theoretical and general goals, it is also possible to achieve other smaller economic objectives. Namely, the mechanism for legal regulation of market competition in Bosnia and Herzegovina has two objectives: the establishment of a single economic space and the fulfilment of one of the conditions for membership in the EU.

127. The following can be said of the mechanism for legal regulation of market competition:

1. it is based on administrative application of law;
2. in relation to prohibited agreements, abuse of dominant position and prohibited concentration, the institute of state aid is regulated by a special act and is under the competence of a separate state body;
3. there are two state bodies with different competences for the application of competition law: the Council of Competition and the State Aid Council;
4. it is of monistic type because:
   a. The Council of Competition is the only body that performs investigative activities and makes decisions on the violation of the Law on Competition in a specific case; that is, there is no separation of investigative procedure from the procedure of decision-making in the specific case.
   b. Even though there are other bodies in charge of enforcement of the Law on State Aid System: the Council of Ministers of Bosnia and Herzegovina, the Government of the FBiH, the Government of the RS and the Government of Brcko District of Bosnia and Herzegovina, which have an obligation to coordinate their activities, the State Aid Council is the only body in charge of making the final decision on the allocation of state aid.
5. as an independent and autonomous body with the status of legal person, the Council of Competition has exclusive authority in deciding on the existence of prohibited competition activities in the market of Bosnia and Herzegovina, in line with the Law on Competition of Bosnia and Herzegovina;

6. the decisions of the Council of Competition are subject to review by the Court of Bosnia and Herzegovina;
7. being a public institution, the State Aid Council has exclusive competence to launch investigations, approve programmes/schemes of state aid and individual state aid, decide on restitution of unlawfully granted state aid, and establish and manage the list of state aid and the list of programmes/schemes of state aid, initiated before the Council was established;
8. even though it is an autonomous and independent body, therefore not a political body, the composition and functioning of the Council are greatly influenced by the political order and are considered to be an example of political determinism in Bosnia and Herzegovina;
9. even though it is a public institution, whose members are appointed from the ranks of economic or legal experts, with a status incompatible with any direct or indirect, permanent or intermittent duty or function which can expose their independence to risk or create a potential conflict of interest, the organisation and activities of the State Aid Council are greatly influenced by political order, which is yet another example of political determinism in Bosnia and Herzegovina;
10. even though its primary duty is to protect the competition and consumer welfare, market protection mechanism of Bosnia and Herzegovina is designed as an instrument for creation of a single economic space of Bosnia and Herzegovina and in order to achieve the conditions for accession to the EU.

128. As can be seen, the application of competition law in Bosnia and Herzegovina is based on administrative enforcement. Article 20 of the Law defines that the Council of Competition, as regards this Law, is an entity with the power to implement the market competition protection. The composition of the Council of Competition includes the offices for competition in the FBiH and RS, as organisational units outside the headquarters of the Council of Competition.

I. Antitrust Authorities

A. Formation, Composition

129. In line with the Law on Competition (Part III), the Council of Competition is an independent body mandated to ensure consistent implementation of the Law in the entire territory of Bosnia and Herzegovina, and it has exclusive competence to decide on the presence of prohibited competition activities in the market of Bosnia and Herzegovina.

130. The Council of Competition has the status of legal person, its headquarters are located in Sarajevo, and the funds for the activities and tasks of the Council of Competition are allocated from the budget of institutions of Bosnia and Herzegovina.

131. Specificity for collective bodies, such as the Council of Competition, is that it is comprised of six members who are appointed for a six-year term of office, with the possibility of one more reappointment.

132. The terms of office of a member of the Council of Competition may terminate before the end of the term only in the cases of: (a) death; (b) resignation; (c) revocation of the term at the proposal of the Council of Competition, for the following reasons: (1) performance of an incompatible duty; (2) unexcused absence from three successive sessions of the Council of Competition; (3) irresponsible, negligent or poor performance.

133. Members of the Council of Competition are selected among recognised experts in certain professional fields and their status is equal to such of administrative judges and incompatible with any direct or indirect, permanent or periodical duty, with the exception of academic activities and work in professional and scientific bodies.

134. The appointment of the members of the Council of Competition is carried out in the following way:

a. three members of the Council of Competition are appointed by the Council of Ministers of Bosnia and Herzegovina, with one member from each of the three constituent nations;
b. two members are appointed by the Government of the FBiH;
c. one member is appointed by the Government of the RS.

At the proposal of the Council of Competition, the Council of Ministers of Bosnia and Herzegovina appoints a president from the ranks of the Council of Competition for a one-year term without the possibility of reappointment during the term of office.

135. Appointment of the Council of Competition is carried out in the following way: three members shall be appointed by the Council of Ministers of Bosnia and Herzegovina, with one member from each of the three constituent nations; two members shall be appointed by the Government of the FBiH and one member shall be appointed by the Government of the RS.

1. Competence

136. In the performance of its activities in accordance with Article 25 of the Law on Competition and the other regulations which regulate the competition policy in BiH, the Council of Competition has the competence to:

a. make by-law acts based on the provisions of this Law and the other by-laws necessary for its implementation;

b. regulate the definitions and calculation methods for specific activity areas, such as banking, insurance, etc.;
c. regulate and provide interpretation of general and specific definitions of the competition terms, as well as the calculation methods for the key competition terms;
d. decide on requests for the initiation and conduct of proceedings;
e. make administrative acts to finalise a proceeding before the Council of Competition;
f. provide opinions and recommendations on any aspect of competition, either ex officio or at the request of the state authorities, undertakings or associations;
g. make internal acts on the internal organisation of the Council of Competition, except for the Rule Book on the internal organisation and systematisation, which is being made with the consent of the Council of Ministers of Bosnia and Herzegovina;
h. initiate the change and amendments to the Law on Competition;
i. propose to the Council of Ministers of Bosnia and Herzegovina the decision on the amount of administrative taxes relating to the practices before the Council of Competition.

In relation to the draft versions and the proposals of the law and the other regulations in the areas which influence market competition and which are to be submitted by the proposal makers, the Council of Competition provides its opinion on their consent to this Law.

In the implementation of this Law and the other regulations in the field of competition, the Council of Competition may establish expert and advisory bodies that may assist in the decision-making process.

The Council of Competition cooperates with international and national organisations and institutions in the area of competition, and, on this basis, it may provide and request all the data and information related to factual and legal issues, also including confidential data. In relation to the exchange of confidential data, legitimate business interests of the undertakings in question must be protected in accordance with the regulations.

The Council of Competition prepares the report on performance and the annual report, which is submitted to the Council of Ministers of Bosnia and Herzegovina for approval. The Council of Competition publishes the annual report in public.

B. Investigating Powers

137. In the proceedings before the Council of Competition, unless regulated differently by the Law on Competition, the Law on Administrative Procedure of Bosnia and Herzegovina ('The Official Gazette of BiH', No. 29/02) is applied.

138. The investigation proceedings in the sense of determining the presence of the infringement of the Law on Competition are conducted by the Council of Competition, which is in charge of making the final decision on the presence of the said infringement.

139. The initiation of proceedings is regulated by Law, according to which the Council of Competition has an active legitimacy to initiate proceedings ex officio if there is reasonable doubt that the practice concerned considerably prevents, restricts and distorts the market competition.

140. Also, in line with Article 27 of the Law on Competition, the Council of Competition can initiate proceedings based on requests that may be submitted by: (a) any legal and natural person having a legal or economic interest; (b) economic chambers, associations of employers and entrepreneurs; (c) consumer associations; (d) executive power bodies in Bosnia and Herzegovina.

141. The Council of Competition makes the resolution (Article 32 of the Law on Competition) to initiate the proceedings, after which it appoints a responsible member of the Council of Competition for managing the proceedings and an official person for carrying out the proceedings and following the instructions of a responsible member of the Council of Competition and regularly submitting the information and the documents collected in the course of the proceedings.

142. Activities that are undertaken by the responsible member of the Council of Competition, an official person and the other staff who provide professional support in the course of the proceedings have the nature of official duties on the basis of written authorisation or ordinance of the Council of Competition. The ordinance contains, in particular, the subject and the purpose of the proceedings and the fines provided for in case of the obstruction or in case of intentional delivery of false, incorrect and misleading information, and the said persons have the duty to show the ordinance prior to the launch of any activities.

143. According to Article 35 of the Law on Competition, in the course of the proceedings, at the request of the Council of Competition, the official parties and other legal and natural persons are obliged to:

a. submit all the required data, such as written statements and documents, disregarding the media they are announced in;
b. ensure direct access to all business premises, movable and immovable property, business books, databases and other documents, without being obstructed by business, state or technical secret;
c. submit all the necessary data from the other persons, which could contribute to solving and explaining certain issues on prevention, limitation or distortion of market competition;
d. ensure the carrying out of all other duties considered necessary for the purpose of stating all the relevant facts to the procedure.

The Law has also defined the possibility of an 'unannounced raid' in order to acquire the necessary information in the investigation stage, and in line with that, Article 35 defines that if there is a reasonable doubt that any of the parties to the proceeding or other persons hold in possession documents or other instruments relevant to the establishing of the substantive facts in the proceedings, the competent court will be requested to issue a written warrant ordering the search of an apartment or premises and the other persons as well as the seizure of items and documents in possession of the parties or other persons.

C. Adjudicating Powers (Ascertaining and Sanctioning)

144. The Council of Competition is the only body competent to decide on the presence of an infringement of the Law on Competition and to impose sanctions for the said infringement.

145. The proceedings on determining the infringement of the Law are conducted before the Council of Competition and this body makes the decision on it within the specified timeframe. When the proceedings are conducted based on the submitted request, the burden of proof rests with the party which submitted the request.

146. A public oral hearing, which is obligatory in all cases with parties of contrary interest, is held before the Council of Competition. There is an exception to this rule when the party against which the proceedings are conducted has issued a written statement and the Council of Competition took a stance that the facts of the case are beyond dispute and that there are no other hindrances preventing the decision from being made. The second case is when any of the summoned parties in the proceedings fails to respond twice to the summons, the Council of Competition will decide without an oral hearing based on its findings, available data and documents.

147. Upon the completion of the proceedings, a responsible member of the Council of Competition submits to the Council of Competition a report on the implemented proceedings and the proposed resolution, while the Council of Competition, at a session, makes the final decision on whether an infringement of this Law has been committed. The final decision on the implementation of the Law can include recommendations and/or sanctions and other measures to the parties in proceedings.

148. Article 43, paragraph 4 of the Law on Competition has left the possibility to the Council of Competition to inform the parties in written form on the content of the decision which it plans to make before the final decision-making.

149. Paragraph 5 of the same Article defines a certain type of legal remedy. At the request of a party or ex officio, the Council of Competition may re-examine its final decision in the following cases: (a) when the facts, used as a basis for the decision, are changed and when those changes are of significant influence on the market competition; (b) when the parties concerned act contrary to the obligations determined by the Council of Competition; (c) when the decision is based on incomplete, incorrect and misleading information provided by the parties.

150. The decisions of the Council of Competition are final and they are delivered to the parties in the proceedings and published in the 'Official Gazette of BiH', official gazettes of entities and the Brcko District of Bosnia and Herzegovina and they have no influence on potential criminal and/or civic responsibility as to which a decision is taken by the competent courts.

151. The legal remedy is defined by the Law on Competition in the form of an administrative dispute before the Court of Bosnia and Herzegovina, within thirty days from the receipt (subjective time limit) or the publication (objective time limit) of such decision.

D. Other Institutional Tasks (Consultancy to Parliament/Government)

152. In the procedure of deciding on the presence of infringements to the Law on Competition, the Council of Competition is independent and does not have an obligation to consult with Parliament or the Government.

153. The only obligation, in the sense of cooperation with other state bodies, is to provide opinions and recommendations on any aspect of the competition at the request of a state body, as well as to provide opinions on the degree of harmonisation of drafts and proposals of other regulations with the Law on Competition, which the nominators have a duty to deliver.

II. Government Direct Enforcement Activities

154. Ministry of Bosnia and Herzegovina and entity ministries have no competences in the sense of the enforcement of the Law on Competition of BiH.

III. Other Administrative Agencies Applying Antitrust Rules

155. The Law on Competition has placed the enforcement of the competition law under exclusive competence of the Council of Competition, but the improving of the competition law on the single market of Bosnia and Herzegovina stipulates not only the assessment of harmonisation of certain regulations and the Law on Competition but also its cooperation with other agencies.

The Council of Competition actively participates and establishes different forms of professional cooperation with regulatory bodies in Bosnia and Herzegovina, (e.g., sectoral regulators – energy, banking, telecommunications) which in their scope of activities perform the appropriate tasks relating to market liberalisation, trying to propose the forms of common activities and cooperation which contribute to the overall level of enforcement of market competition law in Bosnia and Herzegovina and faster introduction of the rules and practices of the EU.

IV. Administrative Fines

156. The Law on Competition foresees fines for the infringement of regulations of the Law by making the distinction between light and severe infringements of the Law.

In line with that, Article 48 defines that the fines for severe infringements of the Law are at most 10% of the value of an undertaking's total annual income earned in the financial year preceding the year when the infringement is committed. According to this Article, severe infringement of the Law exists if an undertaking or a natural person:

a. concludes a prohibited agreement or participates in any other way in an agreement that caused prevention, restriction or distortion of the competition in the sense of Article 4 of this Law;
b. abuses a dominant position as regulated by the Law on Competition;
c. participates in the prohibited concentration of undertakings;
d. fails to act on the decisions made by the Council of Competition and which decides on infringements of the Law and measures to establish the competition;
e. implements concentration without a prior decision on the concentration by the Council of Competition.

Article 49 of the Law on Competition stipulates fines for other infringements of the Law. In line with that, the Council of Competition may impose fines on undertakings which are no bigger than 1% of the value of their total income in the preceding business year, if they:

a. act contrary to the request, in sense of delivering incorrect and misleading information or not providing the necessary information within the set time limit and which is necessary in the course of investigation and determining the state of the facts based on which the Council of Competition makes a decision on the infringement of the Law;
b. fail to notify the intended concentration in a way defined by Law;
c. submit incorrect and misleading information in the process of concentration appraisal, necessary for the notification, assessment and the adoption of the Decision on concentration;
d. fail to act according to the decision or the conclusion of the Council of Competition or written order of the competent court.

In terms of lighter or the so-called other infringements, the Council of Competition may impose fines in the amount ranging from BAM 5,000 to BAM 15,000 on responsible persons of the legal persons.

157. Pursuant to Article 51 of the Law on Competition, the Council of Competition may impose fines on legal and/or natural persons that are not parties to the proceedings, in case they fail to act upon the request or order of the Council of Competition to deliver the requested information, and in particular:

a. on legal persons, an amount ranging from BAM 5,000 and BAM 15,000;
b. on responsible persons of the legal persons, an amount ranging from BAM 1,500 to BAM 3,000;
c. on natural persons, an amount ranging from BAM 1,500 and BAM 3,000.

In 2013, the Council of Competition imposed a fine in amount of BAM 1,500 on the responsible person, Mladen Kapor, in the legal entity 'Udruženje lokalnih radio stanica RS' S. Nemanje 13, Istočno Sarajevo, Bosna i Hercegovina, for non-acting accordingly with the request of the Council of Competition.[50] In 2014, the Council of Competition imposed a fine in amount of BAM 1,500 on the responsible person, Neven Čičko, in the legal entities 'OBN' d.d. Humska 1, Sarajevo, Bosna i Hercegovina, for non-acting accordingly with the request of the Council of Competition, i.e., for non providing the requested data in accordance with Article 35 of the Law on Competition.[51] According to this article, in conducting the proceedings, parties and other legal and natural persons are obliged, upon the request of the Council of Competition or an official person, to provide all necessary information in the form of written submissions or oral statements and provide access to the required information and documents, regardless of the type of media. There have not been fined companies, as legal entities, so far.

158. In order for the regulation to be applied to undertakings, they need to achieve voluntary cooperation with the Council of Competition and present the evidence of importance for the passing of decision on violations to Article 4, paragraph (1) of the Law on Competition, which the Council of Competition did not have available. Also, the Decision defined that the conditional resolution to grant the immunity from fine to an undertaking that submitted the application to be granted immunity, and which was later granted conditional immunity from fine, can be suspended if: (a) they fail to cooperate fully, timely and continuously; (b) they fail to reveal all violations to the Law on Competition in the case they were involved in; (c) they do not ensure fully, truthfully and sincerely all the evidence and information they possess or are under their supervision.

The Council of Competition has made the Decision which established that the undertaking 'BHB Cable TV' d.o.o. Lukavac and undertaking 'ELTA-MT' d.o.o Tuzla, by signing agreement on joint management of cable television network in Lukavac (No. 003/05 dated 19 August 2005) do not prevent, restrict and distort competition in sense of the division of markets or sources of supply in the area of provision of cable distribution of radio and television programme in Lukavac, and repealed the Decision on conditional fine release immunity by the Council of Competition, No. 02-26-6-18-03-II/11 of 29 September 2012. In the Application, undertaking BHB Cable stated that it participated in a prohibited agreement under Article 4 paragraph (1) item c) of the Competition Act (hereinafter 'the Act'), as it has concluded an agreement on the management of cable television network with other cable operator, which stipulates that subscribers are divided by the principle that

50. Decision of the Council of Competition of Bosnia and Herzegovina Number 01-26-3-004-41-II/13.
51. Decision of the Council of Competition of Bosnia and Herzegovina Number 01-26-3-001-214-II/13.

even number of subscribers belong to one cable operator and odd number subscribers to the other. After it was established that all the conditions prescribed by law are met, the Council of Competition, at the 17th session held on 29 September 2011. issued a Decision on conditional immunity from fine No. 02-26-6-018-3-II/11 (hereinafter the Decision), by which the undertaking BHB Cable is conditionally granted immunity from fine for infringement of Article 4 paragraph (1) of the Act. Council of Competition submitted the Decision to the undertaking BHB Cable, and in Act No: 02-26-6-018-4-II/11 of 29 September 2011, requested the submission of complete documentation and data stated in the Application. Since the undertaking, BHB Cable, did not provide the requested documentation, the Council of Competition, in the Act No. 02-26-6-018-5-II/11 of 10 November 2011, reiterated the request for documentation. Undertaking BHB Cable, in submission No. 02-26-6-018-6-II/11 of 14 December 2011, had submitted part of the required documentation, and the Council of Competition, in the Act: 02-26-6-018-7-II/11 of 14 November 2011, requested the submission of additional data.

Undertaking BHB Cable has submitted the required documentation, submission No. 26-6-0188-II/11 of 21 December 2011. Having reviewed all relevant facts and evidence of the parties to the proceedings and other relevant undertakings, the Council of Competition established that the conclusion of the Agreement on the joint management is a common commercial policy. The Agreement is a type of partnership agreement governing the joint ownership and use of the network with the intention of equal network management and service delivery. With regard to the signatories thereof, they do not represent actual competitors in the relevant market, as they offer one service to consumers/subscribers. Council of Competition found that the undertaking BHB Cable and undertaking ELTA- MT in the relevant market have a dominant position, but that the dominant position did not result in unrealistically high cost of services because the analysis of the prices of other cable operators in the city environment have shown that the price of the relevant market town Lukavac is lower than in other parts of the country.

V. Administrative Injunctions and Other Restrictive Orders

159. The Law on Competition does not stipulate the possibility of imposing administrative prohibitions.

160. In relation to the procedural activities under the competence of the Council of Competition in line with the Law (e.g., the decisions on notification of intended concentration, decisions on the assessment of harmonisation of agreement with the provisions of the Law, providing opinions and so on), administrative fees are charged. The payment of administrative fees is prescribed by the Decision on the level of administrative fees in relation to proceedings before the Council of Competition ('The Official Gazette of BiH', No. 30/06), which was adopted by the Council of Ministers at the request of the Council of Competition.

161. The Law on Competition stipulates the possibility of ordering measures necessary for ensuring free market competition in the relevant market.

162. In line with Article 19 of the Law on Competition, the Council of Competition will, ex officio or upon the request of the party by means of a separate decision, propose all indispensable measures aimed at restoring free market competition in the relevant market and set the deadlines for their implementation, in cases when:

a. the concentration concerned has been implemented contrary to the decision of the Council of Competition by which the concentration has been assessed as incompatible;
b. the concentration concerned has been implemented without submittal of a prior notification of concentration, and has as its effect the significant impediment of market competition.

To this end, the Council of Competition may, in particular:

a. order for the shares or share capital acquired to be divested (transferred);
b. prohibit or restrict the realisation of voting rights achieved by the shares or share capital of the undertakings to the concentration, and end the joint venture control.

VI. Interim Measures

163. The Law on Competition stipulates the possibility of imposing interim measures.

164. In line with Article 40 of the Law on Competition, the Council of Competition may decide on interim measures on the basis of the preliminary determined infringements where it deems that particular activities of restriction, prevention or distortion of competition, with the meaning of this Law, represent a risk by creating a direct restraining influence on individual undertakings, or on particular sectors of the economy or consumers' interests.

§2. Civil Enforcement

165. The theory is familiar with two types of private prosecution for the compensation of damages caused by the infringement of the competition law: the accompanying lawsuits, which take place after the body in charge of the protection of competition concludes that there was an infringement of competition law, and individual lawsuits which are submitted without previously determining the infringement of competition in the procedure before the body in charge of competition protection.

166. Public application of law in BiH, meaning the enforcement of the rules of competition by the state, is still relatively new in Bosnia and Herzegovina, while the possibility of submitting private charges due to infringement of the competition law is pretty much untested.

167. The Law on Competition does not define the issue of compensation for damages in the sense that the damage caused by acts and activities which represent the infringement of competition, which was determined by the decision of the Council of Competition, is compensated in the course of the proceedings before the competent court.

168. The charges for indemnity due to infringement of the competition law can be conceptualised as a lawsuit on the basis of delict, in line with the general provisions of the Law on Obligations.

I. Competent Civil Courts

169. The Law on Competition does not stipulate the competence of the court for the issue of indemnity. To date, there has been one civil claim, in 2014, at the Municipal Court in Sarajevo regarding compensation of damages on the basis of distorting competition.[52] The Court partially awarded the claimant the requested amount. The claimant had appealed, so the case has not been final yet.

II. Sanctions

170. The Law does not stipulate the possibility of filing charges for the compensation of damages which resulted from the infringement of the provisions of the Law on Competition or the possibility of imposing civil sanctions.

A. Nullity

171. Even though the civil liability and sanctions are not stipulated for the infringement of the Law on Competition, Article 4, paragraph 2 of the Law on Competition itself declares all agreements prohibited pursuant to paragraph 1 of Article 4 null and void.

B. Damages

172. The Law does not stipulate the possibility of filing charges for the compensation of damages resulting from the infringement of the provisions of the Law on Competition or the possibility of imposing civil sanctions.

---

52. *M.R.M. Export-Import d.o.o. Ljubuški v. ASA AUTO d.o.o. Sarajevo* (No. 65 0 Ps 308254 12 Ps).

C. Interim Measures

173. The Law does not stipulate the possibility of filing charges for the compensation of damages which resulted from the infringement of the provisions of the Law on Competition and the imposition of interim measures in civil proceedings.

§3. Criminal Enforcement

174. The application of competition law in Bosnia and Herzegovina is based on the administrative enforcement, where the protection of the law is performed in proceedings before a specially established state-level independent and autonomous body ('The Official Gazette of BiH', Nos 29/02, 12/04, 88/07, 93/07 and 41/13).

I. Criminal Sanctions for Antitrust Violations

175. The Law on Competition does not stipulate criminal liability and sanctions for the infringement of regulations which prohibit agreements, abuse of a dominant position and concentration which resulted in prevention, restriction and distortion of competition in the single market of Bosnia and Herzegovina.

II. Other Applications of Criminal Law to Relevant Conducts

176. According to the Constitution of Bosnia and Herzegovina, as well as relevant legal regulations, the economic relations in BiH are based on the principles of free competition and business operations, free and open market, movement of goods and capital. For every action against the said principles, the legislator has prescribed criminal sanctions due to their importance and their role in the overall state system.

177. Criminal offences against the economy and payment systems fall under criminal offences where the jurisdiction for regulation is divided between BiH, the entities and the Brcko District of BiH.

178. Criminal offences from the current criminal legislation in BiH which refer to infringements of the code of conduct on the market are:

a. Criminal offence 'Violation of Equality in Performing Economic Activity' is, as such, regulated both at state[53] and entity levels,[54] with the influence on the whole territory of Bosnia and Herzegovina.[55]

---

53. Article 204 of the Criminal Code of Bosnia and Herzegovina (Ch. XVII, Criminal offences against the economy, market integrity and in the area of customs): 'Whoever, by misusing his official or influential position or powers in the institutions of Bosnia and Herzegovina, restricts the free movement of people, goods, services or capital between the entities and among the entities and the Brcko

Article 260 of the Criminal Code of the RS (Chapter XXV, Criminal offences against the economy and the payment system): (1) Whoever, by misusing his official position or authority restricts the free movement of people, goods and capital in the territory of the RS, denies or restricts the right of a business company or another legal person or physical person to engage in the trade and sale of goods and services in the territory of the RS, or puts a business company or another legal person or physical person in an unequal position in relation to other entities regarding the labour conditions or turnover of goods and services, or restricts free exchange of goods and services in the territory of the RS, shall be punished by imprisonment for a term between six months and five years. (2) Any official or responsible person in the RS, who, by misusing his official position or authority, restricts the free movement of people, goods and capital between the entities or between the entities and Brcko District of Bosnia and Herzegovina, denies or restricts the right of a business company or another legal person or physical person to engage in the trade of goods and services in the territory of the other entity or Brcko District of Bosnia and Herzegovina, or puts a business company or another legal person or physical person in an unequal position in relation to other entities regarding the labour conditions or conditions for trade of goods and services between the entities and Brcko District of Bosnia and Herzegovina shall be punished by imprisonment for a term between one and eight years.

Article 235 of the Criminal Code of BD BiH (Chapter XXII, Criminal offences against the economy, business operation and safety of payment transactions): (1) A person, who, by abuse of office, influence or authority, restricts the free flow of

---

District of Bosnia and Herzegovina, denies or restricts the right of a business enterprise or another legal person to engage in the trade and sale of goods and services on the territory of the other entity or Brcko District of Bosnia and Herzegovina, or puts a business enterprise or another legal person in an unequal position in relation to other organisations regarding the conditions for work or turnover of goods and services, or restricts free exchange of goods and services among the entities and Brcko District of Bosnia and Herzegovina, shall be punished by imprisonment for a term between six months and five years.'

54. Article 241 of the Criminal Code of FBiH (Chapter XXII, Criminal offences against the economy trade and security of payment systems): (1) Whoever, by abusing his official or influential position or authority, restricts the free movement of people, goods or capital in the territory of the Federation, denies or restricts the right of a business enterprise or another legal or natural person to engage in the trade and sale of goods and services on the territory of the Federation, or puts a business enterprise or another legal or natural person in an unequal position in relation to other persons regarding the conditions for work or turnover of goods and services, or restricts the free exchange of goods and services in the territory of the Federation, shall be punished by imprisonment for a term between six months and five years.

55. Article 241 of the Criminal Code of FBiH (Chapter XXII, Criminal offences against the economy trade and security of payment systems): (2) An official or responsible person in the Federation who, by misusing his official or influential position or powers, restricts the free movement of people, goods or capital between the Entities and among the Entities and the Brcko District of Bosnia and Herzegovina, denies or restricts the right of a business enterprise or another legal or natural person to engage in the trade and sale of goods and services on the territory of the other Entity or Brčko District of Bosnia and Herzegovina, or puts a business enterprise or another legal or natural person in an unequal position in relation to other persons regarding the conditions for work or turnover of goods and services, or restricts free exchange of goods and services among the Entities and Brčko District of Bosnia and Herzegovina, shall be punished by imprisonment for a term between one and eight years.

people, goods and capital in the territory of the Brcko District, denies or restricts the right of a business enterprise or another legal or physical person to engage in sale of goods and services within the Brcko District, or a person who puts a trading enterprise or another legal or physical person in an unequal position in relation to other persons regarding the working conditions or requirements for engaging in sale of goods and services or restricts a free exchange of goods and services in the Brcko District, shall be sentenced to prison from six months to five years. (2) An office holder or a responsible person in the Brcko District who, by abuse of office, influence or authority, restricts the free flow of people, goods and capital in the territory of the Brcko District, denies or restricts the right of a business enterprise or another legal or physical person to engage in sale of goods and services within the Brcko District, or a person who puts a trading enterprise or another legal or physical person in an unequal position in relation to other persons regarding the working conditions or requirements for engaging in sale of goods and services or restricts a free exchange of goods and services in the Brcko District, shall be sentenced to prison from one to eight years.

179. It can be noticed that the criminal offence is prescribed with the same name in both entities and BD BiH, in somewhat different ways than it is prescribed by Article 204 of the CC BiH. A criminal offence from the Article 204 of the CC BiH can only be committed by an employee of the institutions of BiH, while the criminal offence prescribed by CC FBiH, CC RS and CC BD BiH can be committed in two ways: by different forms of violation of equality in performing economic activities between the given entity and the other entity/BDBiH, and the abuse of official or influential position or powers which affects the equality in the market of entities/ BDBiH.

180. Actions which under the provisions of the CC BiH/CC FBiH/CC BDBiH are considered distortion of equality in the market are laid down alternatively: (1) restrictions of the free flow of people, goods and capital; (2) denial or restriction of the right of a business company or another legal person or physical person to engage in the trade of goods and services in the territory of the other entity or BD BiH; (3) placing a business company or another legal person or physical person in an unequal position in relation to other entities regarding the labour conditions or conditions for trade of goods and services; and (4) restriction of free exchange of goods and services between the entities and BD BiH.

181. In order for this to actually be the case of execution of these criminal offences in the sense of restriction of the free flow of people, goods and capital, its actual restriction must take place. In order for some action to be considered an action that denies or restricts an economic entity or a natural person from engaging in the trade of goods or services, the performing of these activities must be completely disabled or certain difficulties that would lead to the termination of the said activities need to be created. The conditions for free and unobstructed performance of economic activities, as well as free flow of goods, people, capital and services, are initially prescribed by entity laws on business entities, but certain provisions of other laws and by-law acts, which in a direct or indirect way prescribe the said conditions, are also related to this matter. It is necessary to pay attention that the restriction in the free flow of people, goods and capital in the sense of creating restricted possibilities for its operation, rather than completely preventing it, appears as an act of perpetration. Besides that, it is necessary to remind that a certain action may be presented as an act of perpetration in the aforementioned sense; these restrictions simply have to take place due to the act of perpetration.

182. Given the fact that the free flow of people, goods and capital between the entities and BDBiH, protection of the single market, unobstructed business operations and equality of undertakings on the market are trying to be ensured by defining those actions that try to damage the market as criminal offences, the aforementioned can be considered an object of protection. In order for the perpetrator to be criminally liable, it must be determined that there was premeditation present during the perpetration of actions, meaning that the perpetrator was aware that while performing a certain duty, his actions could lead to infringement of equality in performing business operations on the market:

a. Criminal offence 'Creation of a Monopolistic Position in the Market', which is regulated on the level of FBiH,[56] RS[57] and BD BiH.

183. Article 248 of the Criminal Code of Brcko District is identical to Article 253 of the Criminal Code of FBiH.

III. Role of Prosecutors

184. The role of prosecutors in the cases of infringement of Article 204 of the Criminal Code of Bosnia and Herzegovina is assessed in line with the Criminal Procedure Code of Bosnia and Herzegovina.[58]

---

56. Article 253 of the Criminal Code of FBiH prescribes: 'Whoever, in a legal person, enters into an agreement by which another legal or natural person is restrained from the free circulation of goods and services within a determined area or with certain legal or natural persons, or enters into an agreement by which in some other way a monopolistic position in the market for certain legal or natural persons is created, shall be punished by imprisonment for a term between six months and five years.'
57. Article 257 of the Criminal Code of RS prescribes: 'Authorised person in an enterprise or other legal person or self-employed person who, in contravention of law or regulations, enters in an agreement to restrict other legal or natural persons' freedom in the commercial market within a given region or with particular legal or natural persons or enters in an agreement to obtain a monopoly for particular legal or natural persons in the commercial market in some other way and thereby obtains significant property gain or causes significant damage to property of another, shall be punished by imprisonment for a term between six months and five years.'
58. Code of Criminal Procedure of Bosnia and Herzegovina ('The Official Gazette of BiH', Nos 3/03, 32/03, 36/03, 26/04, 63/04, 13/05, 48/05, 46/06, 76/06, 29/07, 32/07, 53/07, 76/07, 15/08, 58/08, 12/09, 16/09, 93/09, 72/13) was imposed by the decision of the High Representative and published in the 'Official Gazette of BiH', No. 3/03. Correction of the imposed Law was published in the 'Official Gazette of BiH'. the text of the Law was adopted by the Parliamentary Assembly of BiH and published in the 'Official Gazette of BiH', No. 37/03.

185. The role of the prosecutor in the cases of infringement of Articles 241 and 253 of the Criminal Code of FBiH is regulated by the Criminal Procedure Code of FBiH.[59]

186. The role of the prosecutor in the cases of infringement of Articles 257 and 260 of the Criminal Code of the RS is regulated by the Criminal Procedure Code of the RS ('The Official Gazette of RS', No. 53/12).

187. The role of the prosecutor in the cases of infringement of Articles 235 and 248 of the Criminal Code of Brcko District is regulated by the Criminal Procedure Code of Brcko District ('The Official Gazette of BD BiH', No. 33/13).

IV. Competent Criminal Courts

188. In cases involving violations of state and entity laws and the laws of the Brcko District, the principle of local, meaning territorial competence is applied.

59. 'Official Gazette of FBiH', No. 35/03 28 Jul. 2003; Amendments, changes and supplements: OG FBiH: No. 37/03; OG FBiH: No. 56/03; OG FBiH: No. 78/04; OG FBiH: No. 28/05; OG FBiH: No. 55/06; OG FBiH: No. 27/07; OG FBiH: No. 53/07; OG FBiH: No. 9/09; OG FBiH: No. 12/10.

Part II. Prohibited Practice

Chapter 1. Restrictive Agreements

§1. Horizontal Agreements

189. According to Article 4 paragraph (1) of the Competition Law of Bosnia and Herzegovina prohibited are agreements, contracts, certain provisions of the agreement or contract, joint actions, explicit and tacit agreements of economic entities, as well as decisions and other acts of economic entities that have aimed at and resulted in prevention, restriction or distortion of market competition in the relevant market, which related to:

a. direct or indirect fixing of selling and purchase prices or any other trade conditions;
b. limit or control on production, markets, technical development or investment;
c. share of markets or sources of supply;
d. application of dissimilar conditions to equivalent transactions with other economic entities, thereby placing them at a competitive disadvantage;
e. conclusion of contracts subject to acceptance by the other parties of additional obligations which, by their nature or according to commercial usage, have no connection with the subject of such contracts.

All those prohibited agreements are void. But there is an exception. According to Article 4 paragraph (3), the agreements are not prohibited if they contribute to improving the production or distribution of goods and/or services within Bosnia and Herzegovina or if they contribute to the promotion of technical or economic progress, allowing consumers a fair share of the resulting benefit which:

a. impose only restriction necessary for the achievement of these objectives;
b. do not allow the exclusion of competition in an essential part of the subject products or services.

190. If the above-mentioned conditions are fulfilled Council of Competition, at the request of one or more parties to the agreement, may issue a decision on individual exemption from the prohibition of agreements. If the Council of Competition within the period of three months does not issue a decision, it is considered that subject agreement is exempted from the prohibition laid down in Article 4. However, the Council of Competition may, ex officio or at the request of a party, already exempted agreement re-examine, if it finds:

a. decision has been made based on incomplete and incorrect data and information;
b. material conditions and facts in the relevant market have been changed substantially;
c. one of the parties in question acts contrary to obligations which are determined by the Council of Competition.

The Council of Competition may, if it finds the violations, cancel, revoke or amend its decision.

191. Individual exemption may contain conditions and prohibitions. Duration of individual exemption is effected for limited period, which as a rule may not exceed five years. This period, at the request of the parties, may be further extended for up to five years, if it is proved that the agreement continues to satisfy the requirements of Article 4 paragraph (3). Request for extension of validity of an individual exemption, the parties shall submit to the Council of Competition no later than four months before the expiry of deadline. Individual exemption is valid from the date of signing the agreement, and when it contains conditions and prohibitions, it is valid from the date of enactment, or the latest from the day of fulfilment of conditions.

192. Article 4 of the Bosnia and Herzegovina Competition Law is probably the most peculiar and controversial provision. At first glance, it seems that this Article is literally copied from the Treaty of European Community (TEC). Which is correct, except for one, small but importance difference. That difference could be considered a *differentia specifica* in comparison to the EU law. As it is stated in Article 4, prohibited are agreements, contracts, certain provisions of the agreement or contract, joint actions, explicit and tacit agreements of economic entities, as well as decisions and other acts of economic entities that have aimed and resulted in prevention, restriction or distortion of market competition in the relevant market. Article 101 Treaty on the Functioning of the European Union (TFEU) (ex 81(1) TEU) does not proscribe both intention and result (consequence), but only one or another condition for the prohibition.

193. As it could be seen, the Bosnia and Herzegovina Competition Act prescribed those conditions (more) strictly than the EU law. It is understandable and logical that as long as there is an agreement that aims to prevent, restrict or distort competition should be considered prohibited. The condition of *causa* has not to be fulfilled as in criminal law. This is an obvious deviation from the EU law since two conditions for prohibited agreement(s) must be fulfilled cumulatively.

194. The question is – why is this the case? Is it just a tippfehler in the text of the Competition Act, an error in translation, or was it made on purpose? If it is made on purpose, why is it so? This specificum is quite idiopathic. It could be seen as the biggest lack of the monopolistic agreements in Bosnia and Herzegovina's law.[60]

195. However, it was interesting and challenging to find out what does the Bosnia and Herzegovina Council of Competition do in cases of determining a prohibition. As it was established as a body with the exclusive competence in making decisions on the presence of prohibited competition practices in the market[61] and having in mind that it is authorised to use the case law of the European Court of Justice and the decisions of the European Commission,[62] it is understandable why the Council of Competition pretends that there are both conditions fulfilled in the case they are not, although this is not often the case. This action could be considered an interpretation of domestic competition law in accordance with EU law. However, it should be changed in future amendments of the Law.

I. Cartels

A. Price Fixing

196. The Competition Act stipulated price fixing as prohibited competitive activity only in one article – Article 4 paragraph (1) issue (a). So, prohibited are agreements, contracts, certain provisions of the agreement or contract, joint actions, explicit and tacit agreements of economic entities, as well as decisions and other acts of economic entities that have aimed at and resulted in prevention, restriction or distortion of market competition in the relevant market, which related to direct or indirect fixing of selling and purchase prices or any other trade conditions.

B. Market/Client Allocation

197. The Competition Act stipulated price fixing as prohibited competitive activity only in one article – Article 4 paragraph (1) issue (b) and (c). So, prohibited are agreements, contracts, certain provisions of the agreement or contract, joint actions, explicit and tacit agreements of economic entities, as well as decisions and other acts of economic entities that have aimed at and resulted in prevention, restriction or distortion of market competition in the relevant market, which related to limit or control on production, markets, technical development or investment; share of markets or sources of supply, application of dissimilar conditions to equivalent transactions with other economic entities, thereby placing them at a competitive disadvantage, conclusion of contracts subject to acceptance by the other parties of additional obligations which, by their nature or according to commercial usage, have no connection with the subject of such contracts.

60. M. Trifković (2006), Određivanje monopolističkih sporazuma u pravima Bosne i Hercegovine i Evropske unije, Pregled, 4/2006, 91.
61. Article 21(1) of the Bosnia and Herzegovina Competition Act.
62. Article 43(7) of the Bosnia and Herzegovina Competition Act.

C. Production/Innovation Limitation

198. The Competition Act does not stipulate any paragraph considering this issue. However, it should be mentioned that a compulsory licence, regulated by Patent Law and Law on Protection of New Plant Variety of Bosnia and Herzegovina, as *legis specialis*.

199. Compulsory or statutory, also known as obligatory licence, is an authorisation granted by the government to apply the patented invention without the permission of the patent holder, which restricts him in the exercise of his exclusive rights guaranteed by the legal system. This will be the case only if the patent holder denies ceasing his rights to economic exploitation or imposing unreasonable conditions for it. A compulsory licence may be granted only if the person filing the request unsuccessfully attempted, within a reasonable period of time, to obtain authorisation from the patent holder for the exploitation of the protected invention on reasonable commercial terms and conditions. A compulsory licence may not be granted if the patent holder proves the existence of legitimate reasons justifying non-exploitation or insufficient exploitation of the protected invention.

200. Usually, the patent holder will be against ceasing know-how, which practically implies that the licensee will work in hostile environment.[63] Understandably, the patent holder has right to be financially compensated.

201. The Patent Law of Bosnia and Herzegovina makes difference between a compulsory and a compulsory licence issued in public interest (public interest compulsory licence, also known as official licence). Public interest compulsory licence is justified only if there are reasons of protection of the public interest or competition law. It may be granted if the exploitation of the invention protected by a patent is necessary due to national emergencies for the purpose of:

a. state security;
b. protection of public interest in the field of health and nutrition;
c. protection and improvement of human environment;
d. special interest in a particular branch of economy or where it is necessary to correct practices determined in a judicial or administrative process to be uncompetitive.

202. According to the Patent Law, a compulsory licensing has to be issued by the Court of Bosnia and Herzegovina, while issuing a public interest compulsory licensing is within jurisdiction of the Council of Ministers of Bosnia and Herzegovina. However, it has not been used in Bosnia and Herzegovina (yet).

63. Bubalo, L., (2013) Institut prinudne licence u međunarodnom, uporednom i bosanskohercehovačkom pravu, Nova pravna revija, p. 62.

D. Group Boycott

203. Group boycott as legal institution in Bosnia and Herzegovina's law has not been regulated as such; thus, it is not applicable in domestic jurisdiction.

E. Collusion on Other Objects

204. Collusion on other objects as legal institution in Bosnia and Herzegovina's law has not been regulated as such; thus, it is not applicable in domestic jurisdiction.

II. Information Exchange Practice

205. Information exchange practice as legal institution in Bosnia and Herzegovina's law has not been regulated as such, and thus is not applicable in domestic jurisdiction.

III. Cooperation Agreements

206. According to Article 7 of the Competition Law, named Block Exemption, the Competition Council adopted in 2005 Regulation on Block Exemption Granted to Certain Categories of Horizontal Agreements (Between Undertakings Operating at The Same Level of Production or Distribution Chain) Relating Particularly to Research, Development and Specialisation Agreements.

207. This Regulation stipulate the conditions for block exemptions granted to certain categories of horizontal agreement, i.e., agreements between undertakings which operate on the same level of production or distribution chain (hereinafter: 'horizontal agreements') relating particularly to research, development and specialisation agreements, set out the restriction and conditions which such agreements may not contain, and other conditions which must be fulfilled in order to satisfy the conditions for exemption from application of the provisions on prohibited agreements set out in Article 4. of the Competition Law.

208. According to the 2011 Regulation on Block Exemption, block exemption shall apply to horizontal agreements entered into between two or more independent undertakings which for the purpose of the agreement operate at the same level of production or distribution chain, and particularly to research and development agreements and specialisation agreements. Accordingly, the block exemption shall not apply to horizontal agreements which do not fulfil the cumulative conditions laid down under Article 4 of the Competition Law and which are not brought into compliance with the Regulation on Block Exemption, as well as horizontal agreements which fall within the scope of any other regulations.

A. Research and Development

209. Research and development agreements are horizontal agreements entered into between two or more independent undertakings which relate to the conditions under which those undertakings pursue:

a. joint research and development of products or processes and joint exploitation of the results of that research and development; or
b. joint exploitation of the results of research and development of products or processes jointly carried out pursuant to a prior agreement between the same undertakings; or
c. joint research and development of products or processes which excludes joint exploitation of the results of that research and development.

This block exemption granted to research and development agreements shall also apply to provisions contained in those agreements which do not constitute the primary object of such agreements, but are directly related to and necessary for their implementation, such as an obligation not to carry out, independently or together with third parties, research and development in the field to which the agreements relate or in a closely connected field during the execution of the agreement.

210. The block exemption for research and development agreement shall apply if the following conditions are met:

a. All participants must have access to the results of the joint research and development for the purpose of further research or exploitation of results. Exceptionally, research institutes, academic bodies or undertakings which supply research and development as a commercial service without normally being active in the exploitation of results may agree to confine their use of the results to the purpose of further research.
b. Each party must be free independently to exploit the results of the joint research and development and any pre-existing know-how necessary for the purpose of such exploitation, when a research and development agreement ensures only joint research and development. Such right to exploitation may be limited to one or technical fields of application, where the parties are not competing undertakings at the time the research and development agreement is concluded. In this context, research and development means the acquisition of know-how relating to products or processes and the carry out of theoretical analysis, systematic studies or experimentation, including experimental production, technical testing of products or processes, and the establishment of the necessary facilities and the acquisition of intellectual property right for the results.
c. Any joint exploitation must relate to results which are protected by intellectual property rights or constitute know-how, which substantially contribute to technical or economic progress, and those results must be decisive for the manufacture of the contract products or the application of the contract processes. Within the meaning of this paragraph, exploitation of results means the production or distribution of the contract products or the application of the contract processes

or the assignment or licensing of intellectual property rights or the transfer of know-how required for such manufacture of the contract products or application of contract processes. Research and development or exploitation of the research and development are carried out jointly where the work involved is carried out by a joint team, organisation or undertaking, or jointly entrusted to a third party, or allocated between the parties to the agreement by way of specialisation in research, development, production or distribution. Contract product means a product which is the subject of the agreement arising out of the joint research and development or manufactured or provided by applying the contract processes. Contract process means a technology or process arising out of the joint research and development.

d. Undertakings charged with manufacture by way of specialisation in production must fulfil orders for supplies from all parties to the agreement, except when the research and development agreements at the same time provide for the joint distribution.

According to the Regulation, know-how means a package of non-patented practical information, resulting from experience and testing, which is secret, substantial and identified. In this context, 'secret' means that the know-how as a body or in the precise configuration and assembly of its components is not generally known or easily accessible. 'Substantial' means that the know-how includes data and information which are indispensable for the manufacture of the contract products or the application of a sufficiently comprehensive manner so as to make it possible to verify that it fulfils the criteria of secrecy and substantiality.

211. When it comes to the duration of block exemption, when the participating undertakings are not competing undertakings, the exemption shall apply for the duration of the research and development. When the results are jointly exploited, the exemption shall continue to apply for seven years from the time the contract products are first put in the relevant market. When two or more of the participating undertakings are competing undertakings, the block exemption for research and development agreements shall apply as it stated, if, at the time when the research and development agreement is entered into force, the combined market share of the participating undertakings does not exceed 25% of the relevant market for the product capable of being improved or that are substitutes for the contract product.

212. After the mentioned period has ended, the block exemption shall continue to apply as long as the combined market share of the participating undertakings does not exceed 25% of the relevant market for the contract products. If this market share is, at the moment of signing the agreement, not more than 25% but subsequently rises above this level without exceeding 30% the block exemption shall continue to apply for a period of two consecutive calendar years following the year in which 25% of the market share is first exceeded. But, if the market share at the moment of signing the agreement is not more than 25% but subsequently rises above 30%, the block exemption shall continue to apply for one calendar year following the year in which the level of 30% of the market share is first exceeded. The benefit of block exemptions may not be combined so as to exceed a period of two years.

213. The market share of the participating undertakings in research and development agreements shall be calculated on the basis of the sales value of the contract products and their substitutes in the market. If the sales value data of the contract products and their substitutes in the market are not available, estimates based on other reliable market information, including the sales volume of the contract products and their substitutes in the relevant market, may be uses to establish the market share of the undertaking concerned. The market share shall be calculated on the basis of data relating to calendar year preceding the conclusion of the agreement.

214. The block exemption shall not apply to research and development agreements which, directly or indirectly, in isolation or in combination with other factors under the control of the parties to the agreement, have as their object:

a. the restriction of the freedom of the participating undertakings to carry out research and development independently or in cooperation with third parties in a field to which the research and development relates or in the cognate field;
b. the prohibition to deny the validity of intellectual property rights which are relevant to the research and development when the research and development is completed or the validity of intellectual property rights which protect the results of the research and development, when the research and development agreement expired, without prejudice to the possibility to provide for the termination of the research and development agreement in the case when one of the party to the agreement denies the validity of such intellectual rights;
c. limitation of the manufacture or sale;
d. fixing prices when selling the contract product to third parties;
e. the restriction of the customers to whom the participating undertakings may sell the contract products, when the period of seven years ends, starting from the time the contract products are first put on the market;
f. the prohibition to make passive sale of the contract products in territories reserved for other parties to the agreements;
g. the prohibition to put the contract products on the market or to pursue an active sales policy of those products in territories reserved for other parties, when the period of seven years ends, starting from the time the contract products are first put on the market;
h. setting the conditions under which the third parties shall not be granted the licences to manufacture the contract product or to apply the contract processes, if the exploitation of the result of the joint research and development by at least one of the parties to the agreement is not provided for or does not take place;
i. setting the conditions under which the demand from users or sellers in their respective territories shall be refused, if they sell the contract products in other territories; or
j. setting of conditions under which it is difficult for the users or sellers to obtain the contract product from other sellers and in particular, to exercise intellectual property rights, or taking measures so as to prevent users or sellers from obtaining, or from putting on the market, the products which have been lawfully put on the market by another party to the agreement or within its consent.

The following provisions contained in research and development agreements shall not be considered as prohibited competition restrictions:

a. setting of production targets in a case when the exploitation of the results includes the joint production of the contract products;
b. setting of sales targets and fixing of prices charged to immediate customers when the exploitation of the results includes the joint distribution of the contract products.

The passive sales mean sales in response to requests from individual customers in other parties' exclusive territories, including delivery of products to such customers, but such responding must not be the result of active sales operations. Passive sales also means the general advertising or promotion in the media or on the internet that reaches customers in other parties' exclusive territories and customers in the respective territories, which is a result of the development in technology and easy access, and therefore it is considered to be a reasonable method of approaching these customers.

215. The active sales mean sales by actively searching for or approaching individual customers or particular customer groups inside another party's exclusive territory, conclusion of individual agreements, taking measures of general presentation of products to those customers, establishing branches, warehouses or organising distribution networks and promotions in that territory. An active approach includes visits, direct and electronic mail to customers, advertisement in the media or other promotions, specifically targeted at those customer groups in the other parties' exclusive territory.

B. Specialisation

216. Specialisation agreements are horizontal agreements entered into between two or more independent undertakings which set the conditions under which those undertakings specialise in the production of products, and such agreements shall be considered:

a. unilateral specialisation agreements, by virtue of which one party to the agreements agrees to cease production of certain products or to refrain from producing those products and to purchase them from a competing undertaking, while the competing undertaking agrees to produce and deliver those products; or
b. mutual (reciprocal) specialisation agreements, by virtue of which two or more parties to the agreement on a reciprocal basis agree to cease or refrain from producing certain but different products and to purchase these products from the other parties to the agreement, who deliver those products; or
c. joint production agreements, by virtue of which two or more parties to the agreement agree to produce a certain product jointly.

The block exemptions granted to specialisation agreements shall also apply to provisions contained in those agreements, which do not constitute the primary object of such agreements, but are directly related to and necessary for their implementation, such as provisions concerning the assignment or use of intellectual property rights. Intellectual property rights in this context include industrial property rights, copyright and neighbouring rights. Participating undertakings in this context are undertakings that are parties to the agreement and undertakings that are connected to them. Competing undertaking in the meaning of the mentioned condition is an undertaking that is active at the same relevant market as an actual competitor or a potential competitor, that is to say an undertaking that would, on realistic grounds, undertake the necessary additional investments or other necessary switching cost structure so that it could enter the relevant market in response to a small but permanent increase in price.

217. The block exemption for specialisation agreement shall apply if the following conditions are met:

a. the parties to the agreement accept an exclusive purchase and/or exclusive supply obligation in the context of a unilateral or reciprocal specialisation agreement or a joint production; or
b. the parties to the agreement do not sell independently the products which are the object of the specialisation, but they take part in joint distribution or agree to appoint a third party to be distributor on an exclusive or non-exclusive basis in the context of a joint production agreement, provided that the third party is not a competing undertaking.

Production in this context means the manufacture of goods or the provision of services and includes production by way of cooperatives or subcontractors. The exclusive distribution obligation means an obligation to supply exclusively the contract product relating to specialisation agreement to the parties to the agreement, i.e., such obligation excludes the possibility of supplying its competing undertaking. The exclusive purchase obligation means an obligation to purchase the product to which the specialisation agreements relate only from the party to the agreement which agrees to supply those products.

218. The block exemption for the specialisation agreements shall apply on condition that the combined market share of the participating undertakings does not exceed 20% in the relevant market. If the market share of the participating undertakings is, at the moment of signing the agreement, not more than 20% but subsequently rises above that level without exceeding 25%, the block exemption shall continue to apply for a period of two consecutive calendar years following the year in which 20% of the market share is first exceeded. If the market share of the participating undertakings is, at the moment of signing the agreement, not more than 20% but subsequently rises above 25%, the block exemption shall continue to apply for one calendar year following the year in which 25% of the market share is first exceeded. The benefit of these block exemptions may not be combined so as to exceed a period of two calendar years.

219. The market share of the participating undertakings to specialisation agreements shall be calculated on the basis of the sales value of the contract products and their substitutes. If the sales value data of the contract product and its substitutes in the market are not available, estimates based on other reliable market information, including market sales volumes of the contract products and their substitutes in the relevant market, may be used to establish the market share of the undertakings concerned. The market share shall be calculated on the basis of data relating to the calendar year preceding the signing of the agreement.

220. The block exemption shall not apply to specialisation agreements which, directly or indirectly, in isolation or in combination with other factors under the control of the parties to the agreement, have restriction with the aim of:

a. fixing prices when selling the products to third parties;
b. limitation of manufacture or sales; or
c. allocation of market or customers.

The following provisions contained in specialisation agreement shall not be considered prohibited competition restrictions:

a. provisions on the agreed amount of products in the context of unilateral or reciprocal specialisation agreements or setting of the capacity and production volume of joint production (joint venture) in the context of a joint production agreement; and
b. the setting of sales targets and the fixing of prices that a production joint venture charges to its immediate customers in the context of the conditions that specialisation agreements must contain.

C. Standardisation

221. Standardisation as legal institution in Bosnia and Herzegovina's law has not been regulated; thus, it is not applicable in domestic jurisdiction.

D. Joint Production

222. Joint production as legal institution in Bosnia and Herzegovina's law has not been regulated; thus, it is not applicable in domestic jurisdiction.

E. Joint Purchasing

223. Joint purchasing as legal institution in Bosnia and Herzegovina's law has not been regulated; thus, it is not applicable in domestic jurisdiction.

F. Joint Selling

224. Joint selling as legal institution in Bosnia and Herzegovina's law has not been regulated; thus, it is not applicable in domestic jurisdiction.

§2. Vertical Agreements

225. As mentioned previously, in a different context, according to Article 7 of the Competition Law, named Block Exemption, the Competition Council adopted in 2006 Regulation on Block Exemption Granted to Certain Categories of Vertical Agreements (Between Undertakings Operating at the Different Levels of Production or Distribution). This Regulation stipulates the conditions for block exemptions granted to certain categories of vertical agreements, i.e., agreements between undertakings which operate at the different levels of production or distribution, restriction or conditions which may be and must be contained herein and other conditions in line with the provisions of Article 7 of the Competition Law. The Regulation regulates four agreements (exclusive distributorship, exclusive dealing, selective distribution and franchising) through general provisions, not separately.

226. Vertical agreements include those agreements or joint ventures between two or more undertakings which operate at different levels of production and distribution chain, relating to the conditions under which the undertakings may purchase, sell or resell particular products or services.

I. Distribution

A. Exclusive Distributorship

227. According to 2006 Regulation on Block Exemption Granted to Certain Categories of Vertical Agreements (Between Undertakings Operating at The Different Levels of Production or Distribution), exclusive distribution agreements are referring to the situations where the supplier undertakes to limit the sale of contract products and/or services to only one selected distributor in a particular territory or to particular group of customers which is exclusively allocated to that distributor.

B. Exclusive Dealing

228. According to 2006 Regulation on Block Exemption Granted to Certain Categories of Vertical Agreements (Between Undertakings Operating at The Different Levels of Production or Distribution), exclusive supply agreements encompass two situations – where the buyer undertakes to purchase the contract products only from one particular supplier and where the supplier undertakes to sell the contract products, either directly or indirectly, only to one buyer in the territory of Bosnia and Herzegovina for the purpose of a specific use or for sale.

C. Selective Distribution

229. According to 2006 Regulation on Block Exemption Granted to Certain Categories of Vertical Agreements (Between Undertakings Operating at The Different Levels of Production or Distribution), selective distribution agreements are referring to the situations where the supplier undertakes to sell the contract products, either directly or indirectly, only to distributors, selected on the basis of transparent, specified criteria and where the distributors undertake not to sell such products to unauthorised distributors.

D. Franchising

230. According to 2006 Regulation on Block Exemption Granted to Certain Categories of Vertical Agreements (Between Undertakings Operating at The Different Levels of Production or Distribution), franchise means agreements where one undertaking (franchisor) provides the other party (franchisee), in return for direct or indirect finance reimbursement, with the right to use the franchise, i.e., the package of intellectual or industrial property rights for manufacture and/or sale purposes of particular products or provision of services. Intellectual or industrial property rights package relates to a trade name and trade mark or signs, know-how, models, designs, copyright, technology knowledge or patents which shall be used for further sale contract products or services to end users. Franchise agreements are not applied to industrial (technology) franchise agreements relating to manufacture of products or technological process in the manufacture of such products.

231. Agreements containing provisions which relate to the assignment of intellectual property rights to the buyer or exercise of those rights by the buyer, provided that those provisions do not constitute the primary object of such agreements and that they are directly related to the use, sale or resale of contact products or services by the buyer or its customers.

II. Technology Licensing

A. Patent Licensing

232. According to Article 70 (Transfer of rights and licence) of the Patent Law of Bosnia and Herzegovina,[64] a patent may be the subject of a total or partial transfer of rights, as well as the subject of a licence agreement. The Licence Agreement gives the right to use the protected invention.

64. 'Official Gazette of BiH', No. 53/10.

233. The contract on transfer of rights, as well as the licence agreement, shall be concluded under the conditions and in the manner prescribed by the special regulations governing the issue of mandatory relations. The conclusion of the transfer of rights and licence agreements requires the consent of all holders of rights.

234. The transfer of rights and licences shall be effective against third parties from the date of registration in the Register of Patent Applications or the Register of Patents. The entry of the licence in the Register shall be made at the request of one of the parties and published in the official gazette. The provisions of this Article shall apply *mutatis mutandis* to the conclusion of transit contracts, as well as licensing agreements, which are subject to the rights of the patent application, a consensual patent and supplementary protection certificates.

235. The decision rejecting the application for the grant of a patent does not have a retroactive effect on the agreement on transfer of rights in the application, and the licence agreement, if and to the extent that the contract is executed, unless the transferor or licensor acted negligently.

236. The entry in the Register and the publication shall be regulated by the implementing regulation.

B. Trademark Licensing

237. According to Article 60 (Licence and franchise) of the Trademark Law of Bosnia and Herzegovina, the holder of a trademark or the applicant may license agreement to cede the right to use a trademark or the rights conferred by the application, and for all or only for some types of goods or services.[65]

238. The licence contract shall be made in writing and must include: an indication of the parties, the number of trademarks of the application number, the duration of the licence, the goods or services for which the licence is given the scope of the licence. The licence contract shall be registered in the relevant register at the request of the trademark holder, the applicant or the acquirer of rights.

239. Entering the licence agreement in the appropriate register of legal effect on third parties from the date of enrolment. The Intellectual Law Protection Institute shall issue a decision on entering the licence agreement in the appropriate register. A collective trademark and trademark guarantees cannot be the subject of licence agreement.

240. The provisions of this Article relating to the licence agreement shall apply accordingly to the franchise agreement.

---

65. 'Official Gazette of BiH', No. 53/10.

241. According to Article 61 of the same Law, the Intellectual Law Protection Institute will publish in the official gazette the transfer, licence registered in the register.

C. Know-How and Trade Secret Licensing

242. According to Article 7 of the Competition Law, named Block Exemption, the Competition Council adopted in 2005 Regulation on Block Exemption Granted to Certain Categories of Technology Transfer Agreements (Licence and Know-How).

243. This Regulation stipulates the conditions for block exemption granted to certain categories of technology transfer agreements (licence agreement and know-how agreements) set out conditions which such agreements may not contain, and other conditions which must be fulfilled in order to satisfy the conditions for block exemption from application of those agreements from application of the provision on prohibited agreements set out in the Competition Law.

III. Block Exemption

A. Applicability of the Block Exemption

244. As stated in Article 2 of The Regulation on Block Exemptions Granted to Certain Categories of Technology Transfer Agreements, block exemption shall apply to technology transfer agreements, as set in the Competition Law, entered into between two undertakings permitting the production of the contract products, including the agreements permitting, besides the production, more than one level of trade.

245. A technology transfer agreements means a patent licensing agreement, licensing agreement on technological knowledge and experience (know-how), a software copyright licensing agreement or a combined patent licensing agreement, licensing agreement on technological knowledge and experience (know-how) or software copyright licensing agreement, including any such agreement containing provisions which relate to the sale and purchase of products or which relate to the licensing of other intellectual property rights and the assignment of intellectual property rights, provided that those provisions do not constitute the primary object of those agreement and that they are directly related to the production of the contract product.

246. The technology transfer agreement means also an agreement on assignment of patents, licensing agreement on technological knowledge and experience (know-how), software copyright or combination thereof in a case where the part of the risk associated with the exploitation of the technology remains with the assignor, in particular where the sum payable in consideration of the assignment of technology is dependent on the income earned by the assignee in respect of products produced with the assigned technology, the quantity of such products produced or the number of operations carried out employing that technology.

247. Licensing agreement on technological knowledge and experience (know-how) in this context means a package of non-patented practical information, resulting from experience and testing, which is secret, substantial and identified.

248. 'Secret' means that the know-how package as a body or in the precise configuration and assembly of its component is not generally known or easily accessible.

249. 'Substantial' means that the know-how includes data, or information which is indispensable and useful for production of the contract products.

250. 'Identified' means that the know-how is to be described in a sufficiently comprehensive manner so as to make it possible to verify that it fulfilled the criteria of secrecy and substantiality.

251. Intellectual property rights are industrial property rights, know-how, copyrights and neighbouring rights.

252. Patent means patents, requests for consensual patent licensing, industrial designs, topographies of semiconductor products, supplementary protection certificated for medical products or other products for which such supplementary protection certificates may be obtained and plant breeder's certificates.

253. Contract product means product produced with the licensed technology and/or product in which such technology has been incorporated.

254. Undertakings – party to the agreement, that is to say, a licensor and licensee, include also their connected undertakings.

B. Inapplicability of Block Exemption

255. As for exemptions, the following agreements may not be excluded from prohibition according to the provisions of the Regulation on Block Exemptions Granted to Certain Categories of Technology Transfer Agreements:

a. technology transfer agreements which do not fulfil the cumulative conditions laid down under Article 8 of the Competition Law and which have not been brought into compliance with the Regulation on Block Exemptions Granted to Certain Categories of Technology Transfer Agreements;

b. technology transfer agreements which fall within the scope of any other regulation pursuant to the provisions of Article 7 of the Competition Law.

Conditions that agreements must contain and other conditions for exemption

IV. Market Share

256.

1. where the parties to the agreement are competing parties, the block exemption provided for in Article 2 of the Regulation Block Exemptions Granted to Certain Categories of Technology Transfer Agreements shall apply on condition that total market share of the parties to the agreement does not exceed 20% on the defined relevant technology and product market. Competing undertakings shall be considered actual competitors in the relevant technology market if they compete in the relevant technology market by assigning licences for substitute technologies without infringing intellectual property rights of other undertakings. Accordingly, undertakings shall be considered actual competitors in the relevant product market which are both active in the relevant product and geographic market in which the contract products are sold without infringing each other's intellectual property rights. Potential competitors in the relevant technology and relevant product market must be undertakings which would, on realistic grounds, undertake necessary additional investments or other necessary switching costs so that they could timely enter, without infringing each other's intellectual property rights, that relevant market in response to a small and permanent increase in prices.
2. where the partied to the agreement are not competing partied, the block exemption provided for in Article 2 of The Regulation on Block Exemptions Granted to Certain Categories of Technology Transfer Agreements shall apply on condition that market share of each of the parties to the agreement does not exceed 30% on the defined relevant technology and product market.
3. for the purpose of the above-mentioned conditions, the market share of the parties to the agreement in the relevant technology market is defined in terms of the presence of the licensed technology in the relevant product market.

A. Calculation of the Market Share

257. The market share of the parties to technology transfer agreement shall be calculated on the basis of the market sales value of the contract product and its substitutes. If the market sales value data concerned is not available, estimates based on other reliable market information, including market sales volumes of the contract products and their substitutes in the relevant market, may be used to establish the market share of the parties to the agreement. The market share shall be calculated on the basis of data relating to the calendar year preceding the conclusion of the agreement. The market share shall include the market share of the respective affiliated companies realised as explained above.

258. The licensor's market share in the relevant technology market shall include the combined market shares of all its licensees calculated on the basis of the sales value data of products incorporating the licensed technology and this for each relevant market separately. When the parties to the agreement are competitors in the relevant technology market, sales value data of products incorporating the licensed technology includes the sales value data of the products incorporating the licensee's own technology. In the case of new technologies being incorporated in new products which have not yet been sold on the market, the market share of the parties to the agreement shall be deemed zero in the technology-relevant market until the sale of new products starts. The market share of both parties to the agreement in the relevant product market shall not take into account the sale value of other licensees, not parties to the agreement in question. The market share of the licensee in the relevant product market includes sale value data of products incorporating the licensed technology and the sale value data of their substitutes. If the licensor is also a supplier of products in the relevant market, then the licensor's market share in that market is calculated on the basis of the sale value data of products.

V. Duration of Block Exemption

259. The block exemption for technology transfer agreement, according to the Regulation Block Exemptions Granted to Certain Categories of Technology Transfer Agreements, shall apply for as long as the intellectual property right in the licensed technology exists, that is to say, until the intellectual property rights expire, lapse or are declared invalid. The block exemption for know-how agreements shall apply for as long as the know-how remains secret, except in the event where the know-how becomes publicly known as a result of action by licensee, in which case block exemption shall apply for the duration of the agreement.

260. When the combined market share of the parties to the agreement, which are competing undertakings in the relevant market, initially does not exceed 20% but subsequently rises above that level, the block exemption shall continue to apply for a period of two consecutive calendar years following the year in which the 20% market share was first exceeded. When the combined market share of the parties to the agreement, which are competing undertakings in the relevant market, initially does not exceed 30% but subsequently rises above that level, the block exemption shall continue to apply for a period of two consecutive calendar years following the year in which the 30% market share was first exceeded.

VI. Hardcore Restrictions Within Agreements Between Competing Undertakings

261. Where the parties to the agreement are competing undertakings, the block exemption shall not apply to agreements which, directly or indirectly, in isolation or in combination with other factors under the control of the parties, have as their object:

a. the restriction of the parties' ability to determine the sale prices of product and then selling them to third parties;
b. the limitation of production, except the limitations on the production of contact products, imposed on the licensee in non-reciprocal agreement or imposed on only one of the licensees in the reciprocal agreement;
c. the allocation of markets or allocation of customers into groups, except for the obligation provided in the Regulation;
d. the restriction of the licensee's right to exploit its own technology or the restriction of the ability of any of the parties to the agreement to carry out research and development, unless such restriction is indispensable to prevent the disclosure of the licensed know-how to third parties.

The above-mentioned allocation of markets or allocation of customers into groups shall not be considered a hardcore restriction of the market competition in the case of:

a. the obligation on the licensee to produce with the licensed technology only within one or more technical fields of use or one or more product markets;
b. the obligation on the licensor and/or licensee, in non-reciprocal agreement, not to produce with the licensed technology within one or more technical fields of use or within one or more product markets or within one or more exclusive territories reserved for the other party to the agreement;
c. the obligation on the licensor not to assign the licence for the said technology to another licensee in a particular territory;
d. the restriction, in non-reciprocal agreement, of active and/or passive sales by the licensee and/or the licensor into the exclusive territory or to the exclusive customer group reserved for the other party to the agreement;
e. the restriction, in a non-reciprocal agreement, of active sales by the licensee into the exclusive territory or to the exclusive customer group allocated by the licensor to another licensee, provided the latter was not a competing undertaking of the licensor in the relevant market at the time of achievement of its own licence;
f. the obligation on the licensee to produce the contract products only for its own use, provided that licensee is not restricted in selling the contract products actively and passively as spare parts for its own products;
g. the obligation on the licensee, in a non-reciprocal agreement, to produce the contract product exclusively for a particular customer, where the licence is assigned for the purpose of creating an alternative source of supply for the customer.

Chapter 2. Dominant Undertakings' Prohibited Practices

262. The categories of dominant position in Bosnia and Herzegovina's competition law are regulated by the Regulation on the Definition of Categories of Dominant Position, adopted in 2006. This Regulation defines the categories, conditions and methods of determination of a dominant position of undertakings, and criteria on abuse of dominant position in the relevant market of products and services of Bosnia and Herzegovina. In addition to the Competition Act of Bosnia and Herzegovina and the Regulation on Definition of Categories of Dominant Position, the Council of Competition may use regulations and case law of the European Court and decisions of the European Commission for the purpose of determination of dominant position for particular cases.

263. According to the Regulation, an undertaking has dominant position in the relevant market of products or services, when, due to its market power, it can behave and operate largely independent of actual potential competitors, buyers, consumers or suppliers, and this restricts or prevents efficient competition. An undertaking has a dominant position in the relevant market of products or services, if there is no competition or if existing competition is insignificant.

§1. Determination of Market Power

264. An undertaking is not dominant in the relevant market of products and services if its market power is not significant. An undertaking has significant market power in the relevant market in relation to actual or potential competitors, particularly regarding the following criteria:

a. market share (scale of sale and purchase in the relevant market of products or services; financial power or product capacities);
b. structure of the relevant market and economic relations with competitors;
c. ability to maintain the prices above the competition level (restricts production and quality);
d. access to supply sources (raw materials) or distribution channels;
e. vertical integration levels of the relevant market;
f. economic regulators, investment obstacles for potential undertakings to enter/exit the relevant market;
g. technological advantages, patents, intellectual or industrial property rights and similar rights.

§2. Abuse of Dominant Position

265. As a rule, a dominant position of an undertaking in the relevant market is not prohibited. Any abuse of dominant position in the relevant market through the operation of undertakings, with the goal and consequence of exclusion or 'closure' of the market to potential competitors, i.e., restriction or distortion of efficient market competition, is prohibited. Abuse of dominant position in the relevant market solely exists in those cases when an undertaking conducts unilateral operation on its own initiative. Two or more undertakings may be dominant (collective dominance) in the relevant market (ex., structural connection, joint policy).

§3. Methods to Determine Dominant Position

266. Dominant position of an undertaking, depending on case in question, can be determined in the whole market of Bosnia and Herzegovina or in its significant part. Methods to determine dominant position also include definition of relevant market (and product or service supply and demand conditions, as well as a substitute product on the market) and ratio of market shares of the undertakings, present in the relevant market (taking into consideration changes within a certain time period).

§4. Market Share of Undertaking

267. It is assumed that an undertaking is dominant in the relevant market of products or services, if its market share exceeds 40%. An undertaking may be dominant if its market share is less than 40% providing other indicators (e.g., weak position and small market share of the existing competitors, serious barriers to enter the relevant market for other undertakings) prove its dominant position. It is assumed that more undertakings have dominant position in the market of goods and/or services, if two or three undertakings have a joint market share of 60% in the relevant market. It is assumed that more undertakings have dominant position in the market of goods and/or services, if four or five undertakings have a joint market share of 80% in the relevant market.

§5. Forms of the Abuse of Dominance

268. The abuse of dominance of one or more undertakings (collective dominance) is considered follows:

a. price discrimination (different prices) of a certain product or service in the different relevant geographic markets;
b. permanent supply and sale of products and services to buyers at low prices, with the consequences of diverting buyers to purchase similar products or services from competing suppliers ('loyal'-targeted sale discounts or secret discounts);
c. fixing a price of the products or service below the production costs with the view to eliminating the competitors;
d. unjustified cancellation or reduction of the production or sale of products or services with negative consequences for consumers;

e. production and market limitations as result of exclusive agreements (special rebates, discounts, financial benefits);
f. putting conditions on buyers to buy additional products or services together with the main product or services;
g. ability of an undertaking to determine conditions in the relevant market regarding its supply and demand, which enables unjustified profit increase;
h. refuse the access for other undertakings, with a reasonable financial charge, to facilities, equipment, relocated network or other infrastructure facilitates, owned or used by the dominant undertaking, if other undertakings are not able, due to legal or other reasons, to operate in the same market of the dominant undertaking, without possibility to use the same capacities/equipment and in if dominant undertaking does not prove that such collective use is not practicable due to operational technical or other reasons or that such use may not be asked from them.

Chapter 3. Concentrations

§1. Joint Ventures

269. The Competition Act does not regulate these kinds of mergers as such. However, the Competition Act's provisions are the applicable law for the above-mentioned kinds of mergers.

Concentration, pursuant to the Competition Act, is deemed to be:

a. joining or merger of independent economic entities or parts of economic entities;
b. the acquisition of control or prevailing influence of one or more economic entities over other economic entities, or over other economic entities or a part of other economic entity, or the parts of other economic entities, as it is:
   1. acquisition by purchasing the majority of shares or share capital; or
   2. acquisition of majority of voting rights; or
   3. otherwise, in accordance with the provisions of the laws governing the establishment of economic entities and their management;
   4. joint venture on a long-lasting basis, of two or more independent economic entities, acting as an independent economic entity.

Acquisition of control can be achieved through exercise of a right, by concluding agreements or by other means by which one or more economic entities, whether separately, either jointly, taking into account all legal and factual circumstances, acquire the possibility of exercising a dominant influence over one or more economic entities.

Prohibited are the concentrations of economic entities, which as a result have a significant distortion of the efficient market competition, in the entire market of Bosnia and Herzegovina or its significant part, especially those which create new or strengthen an existing dominant position.

According to the Competition Act, the following shall not be considered concentration:

a. when banking and other financial institutions or insurance companies, in their regular operations, temporarily acquire shares with the intention of reselling them and put them on sale within the twelve months, and if, within a specified period, ownership of the shares is not used in a way to affect the competitive behaviour of the legal entity, or do not take measures which distort, restrict or prevent market competition. Council of Competition may extend the deadline at the request of a party if an economic entity proves that transaction cannot be implemented within the determined period;
b. when it comes to acquiring control over the economic entity by the person who performs the function of bankruptcy or liquidation manager in terms of the law on bankruptcy and liquidation;

c. when the joint venture is aimed at coordination of market activities between two or more economic entities which retain their independence, in which case the joint venture will be assessed in accordance with the provisions on prohibited competitive activities.

Part III. Administrative Procedure

Chapter 1. Administrative Investigations Before the Antitrust Authority

§1. Initiative

270. The Law on Competition failed to specify the possibility that would enable the professional services or the members of the Council of Competition to conduct certain investigative activities before the launch of official proceedings.

271. With the goal of promoting the quality of work and improving the efficiency and preparation of sessions, the Expert Collegium of the Council of Competition is held. The Expert Collegium serves to discuss the progress of proceedings in different cases, all issues concerning the preparation of sessions, as well as all other current issues which refer to the management and the method of operations of the Council of Competition. The tasks and assignments from under the competence of the Council of Competition are performed by the six members of the Council of Competition, professional service of the Council of Competition, as the basic organisational unit, which performs the tasks and assignments in the headquarters of the Council of Competition, as well as through internal organisational units located outside the headquarters of the Council of Competition in the Federation of BiH and the RS.[66]

272. As it was stated before, the proceedings are launched ex officio or after the initiative of persons who have active legitimacy to launch proceedings when the Council of Competition makes a decision on it.

I. General Sectors Inquiries

273. Within its everyday activities, and in line with the competences specified by Article 25 of the Law on Competition, the Council of Competition provides opinions and recommendations on any aspect of competition, ex officio or at the request

66. Bosnia and Herzegovina, the Council of Competition of BiH, 'Annual Report on the Operations of the Council of Competition in 2012' pp. 5–7.

of a state body, undertakings or associations. By monitoring the situation in the market in Bosnia and Herzegovina, gathering and analysing the comprehensive information from the business community, it is possible to learn of findings which represent the initial basis for the launch of an investigation against a specific undertaking in the case of infringement of the Law on Competition.

II. Ex Officio Investigations

274. If information comes to light that there is a reasonable doubt that there has been an infringement of the Law on Competition, the Council of Competition will act ex officio and initiate the proceedings, as well as make an official decision on it.

III. Complaints

275. The proceedings can be launched based on the demand of participants on the market, meaning legal and natural persons that have economic interest, chambers of commerce, associations and executive bodies.

276. The request to initiate the proceedings before the Council of Competition must contain:

a. the name of the seat of the legal person concerned, or the name and surname and address of the authorised natural person – the applicant;
b. relevant data by means of which it may be established against whom the request is being made;
c. description of facts of the case, practice and circumstances which led to the applicant's request.

Together with the request for initiation of the proceedings, the applicant may enclose, in particular:

a. Relevant documents and other available evidence which prove the allegations of the infringement of the provisions of the Law;
b. evaluation of the relevant market;
c. evaluation of the market share of the applicant and the market share of the competitors in the market;
d. court record certificate, work permit or other relevant documents proving the applicant's registration;
e. the annual report, financial reports and the other accounting documents of the applicant for the financial year preceding the submittal of the request.

After analysing the allegations underlined in the request to initiate the proceedings and determining whether there are grounds to initiate the proceedings, the

Council of Competition of BiH will have thirty days to reach a resolution to initiate the proceedings. The appeal against the resolution to initiate the proceedings is not allowed.

§2. POWERS

277. In order to make the right decision on the infringement of the Law on Competition and to deliver the proper sanction in case the said infringement exists, the Council of Competition must collect evidence and information which will be used as basis to determine the state of facts. The information can be contained in the request (whose authenticity should be verified by the Council of Competition) or based on the Council's investigative 'powers' specified by Article 35 of the Law on Competition. If there is a reasonable doubt that any of the parties to the proceeding or other persons hold in possession documents or other instruments relevant to the establishing of the substantive facts in the proceedings, and they do not want to produce these documents for inspection, the competent court shall be requested to issue a written warrant ordering the search of an apartment or premises and the other persons as well as the seizure of items and documents in possession of the parties or other persons. This implies the potential use of the '*dawn raid*' institute in the competition law of BiH.

I. Requests for Information

278. In line with Article 35, the Council of Competition can request all and any piece of information from the parties to the proceedings and every legal and natural person who can presumably be in possession of information of importance to determine the state of facts and make a decision. More on this can be found in section I: Antitrust Authorities; B; Investigating Powers.

279. At the same time, the members of the Council of Competition, the official persons and the other staff are obliged to keep business secret, irrespective of the way they come to know it, and the obligation of the business secret also continues to be in effect after expiry of their engagement with this body.

280. Business secret is particularly considered to be:

a. all which is defined to be a business secret by the Law or other regulations;
b. all which is defined, on the basis of the law and other documents, to be a business secret or business secret of parties in the procedure or other persons;
c. all which is particularly defined by the parties in the procedure or other persons as business secret.

281. As an exception from the regulations, the data and documents which have been made accessible to the general public in any way, or published pursuant to specific regulations, will not be considered a business secret.

II. Investigating and Search Powers

282. The Council of Competition is the only competent body in charge of investigating and collecting the evidence in the cases of infringement of the Law on Competition, meaning the determining of anti-corruption activities. Just how big the investigative power or competence is can be seen in Article 35 (which was elaborated earlier). Article 35, paragraph 1 of the Law on Competition stipulates the 'announced inspection', in the sense that the Council of Competition can ask through a very formal request to receive all required data regardless of the media they are announced and regardless of the fact that the information in question represents technical, business or state secrets. Extensive interpretation of item 2, paragraph 1 of Article 35 of the Law on Competition brings to a conclusion that the Council of Competition has the authority to have an insight into all movable and immovable property for which it is important to send a timely request which needs to contain the legal basis, subject matter and purpose of the request, limitation period for implementation and the penalties for refusal to act according to the request. However, in line with paragraph 2 of the same Article, when there is a reasonable doubt that any of the parties to the proceeding or other persons hold in possession information relevant to the establishing of the substantive facts in the proceedings, and after refusing to act on a written order by the competent court, the Council of Competition can carry out the search of an apartment or premises and the other persons as well as the seizure of items and documents in possession of the parties or other persons. In practice, this means that the Council of Competition would have the possibility to perform unannounced inspections and searches (dawn raids) of accounts and accounting records, databases, books, correspondence and other business documents, private bags, pockets, electronic calendars, mobile phones and text messages.

III. Cooperation with Other State Institutions

283. The Law on Competition did not specify the obligation of cooperation with other state bodies and institutions of Bosnia and Herzegovina in terms of investigations of infringements of the Law on Competition. However, with the goal to protect and promote the competition in the market of Bosnia and Herzegovina, the Council of Competition performs activities aimed at the establishment and improvement of cooperation with other state bodies and institutions of Bosnia and Herzegovina, and especially with the regulatory bodies at state and entity level, State Electricity Regulatory Commission of Bosnia and Herzegovina, Communications Regulatory Agency of Bosnia and Herzegovina, banking agencies of the Federation of BiH and the RS and so on.[67]

284. The Council of Competition participates with great intensity in the legal protection of consumers, that is, its acts do not allow the prohibited competition activities between undertakings, thus ensuring that the prices of goods and services

67. Report on the Operations of the Council of Competition of Bosnia and Herzegovina in 2012.

are not monopolistic, dominant or any other form of prohibited competition activities, but the legalities of the market in BiH. Also, through its representative in the Consumer Protection Council of BiH, the Council of Competition has a significant role in the improvement and promotion of consumer protection.

285. Significant portion of activities of the Council of Competition is directed towards the development of cooperation with international institutions and organisations – primarily with the European Commission and its bodies, as well as with the OECD, European Bank for Reconstruction and Development (EBRD) and so on. Also, in terms of bilateral relations, cooperation was established with the bodies for market competition from Bulgaria, Croatia, Macedonia, Montenegro, Serbia, Slovenia and other European states. The Council of Competition is also a member of the International Competition Network.

286. In line with the Council of Competition's 2012 Annual Report, the Council of Competition has worked on cooperation and improvement of cooperation with international institutions and organisations, such as the ICN (International Competition Network), OECD, meaning RCC (Regional Competition Organisation), which is in composition of the OECD.

287. In this period, a new mechanism of cooperation was established with the Bulgarian competition authority, which, together with the support of UNCTAD (United Nations Conference on Trade and Development), has established a new regional competitors initiative entitled Sofia Competition Forum, and the Council of Competition supported it as well by signing the Sofia Statement at the constituent conference in November 2012.

288. With the goal of strengthening the regional cooperation in the field of protection of competition in the sector of energy between the surrounding countries, the Secretariat of the Energy Community organised a seminar in Vienna, where the representatives of all competition bodies, participating countries (Albania, Austria, Bosnia and Herzegovina, Bulgaria, Croatia, Estonia, Georgia, Kosovo, Macedonia, Moldavia, Serbia and Ukraine) and the representative of the Secretariat of the Energy Community signed a Joint Declaration on the establishment of a network of competition bodies in the field of energy.

§3. Right of Defence

289. 'The right of defence' is guaranteed from the initiation of proceedings, where Article 33 defines that the Council of Competition has a duty to deliver an answer to the request for the institution of the proceedings to the party against which the procedure has been made, and to the persons established to have the status of a party in the proceedings.

290. The institute of oral hearing, which, in line with Article 39 of the Law on Competition, is obligatory in all cases with parties of contrary interest, is a guaranteed right to every party to the procedure to state its opinion on the allegations from the opponent's side and the arguable state of facts.

I. Content and Notification of Opening Decisions

291. Article 32 of the Law on Competition has specified an obligation for the Council of Competition to make the Resolution authorising the institution of the proceedings, which is both a public and an official decision, meaning an act. Resolution authorising the institution of the proceedings contains, in particular:

a. reference to the related case;
b. provisions of this Law pursuant to which the proceedings have been instituted;
c. the request for submittal of the relevant documentation.

According to the said Article, the Council of Competition is obliged to make a resolution authorising the institution of the proceedings within thirty days upon the receipt of complete and adequate request, and no appeals against the resolution on the institution of the proceedings are allowed.

II. Proceedings: Hearings, Access to File, Briefs

292. As stated before, Article 39 of the Law on Competition determines the obligation of holding an oral hearing in all cases with parties of contrary interest in the proceeding before the Council of Competition and when that action is considered to be useful.

293. The Law also stipulated an exception which refers to the situation in which one of the parties issued a written statement saying that the state of facts is not arguable and that there are no other obstacles to the passing of the solution, which means that the resolution can be reached even without holding an oral hearing.

294. In line with Article 37 of the Law on Competition, the parties to the proceedings before the Council of Competition have the right of access to case files.

295. At a party's request, the Council of Competition shall make a copy of record or single documents delivered by the other parties. Requests for access to the documents are submitted in written form to the Council of Competition, which then sets the date for access to documents within eight days period from the day when the request was received.

296. As an exception to this, the Law has determined that the documents or drafts of the decisions of the Council of Competition, reports and minutes of the sessions of the Council of Competition, internal instructions and notes on the case, as well as the other documents considered an official secret pursuant to the Law, may neither be inspected nor photocopied.

III. Final Hearing and Decision

297. Upon the completion of the proceedings, a responsible member of the Council of Competition submits to the Council of Competition a report on the implemented proceedings and proposals for the decision.

298. At a session, the Council of Competition makes the final decision on whether an infringement of this Law has been committed, and it can include recommendations and/or sanctions and other measures to the parties in proceedings.

299. Before the final decision-making, the Council of Competition may inform the parties in written form on the content of the decision which shall be made.

300. At the request of a party or ex officio, the Council of Competition may re-examine its final decision in the following cases:

a. when the facts, used as a basis for the decision, are changed and when those changes are of significant influence on the market competition;
b. when the parties concerned act contrary to the obligations determined by the Council of Competition;
c. when the decision is based on incomplete, incorrect and misleading information provided by the parties.

Decisions of the Council of Competition are delivered to the parties to the proceedings and published in the 'Official Gazette of BiH', in the official gazettes of the entities and the Brcko District of Bosnia and Herzegovina. In the decisions laid down in paragraph 1 of this Article, the Council of Competition revealed the names of the parties to the proceedings and the main decision content, including set penalties, and it will also take account of the legitimate interests of undertakings in relation to the protection of their business secrets.

Chapter 2. Merger Control

§1. Preliminary Filing Obligations

301. The obligation to report concentrations and financial thresholds for its existence.

302. Article 14 of the Law on Competition specifies the total income as the threshold for the control of concentration. Pursuant to paragraph 1 of Article 14 of the Law on Competition, the intended concentration is obliged to be notified by parties to the concentration if the following conditions are met:

a. the total income of all the undertakings-parties to the concentration, realised by the sale of goods and/or services in the global market, amounts to BAM 100 million, according to the balance sheet of the financial year preceding the concentration; and
b. the total income of each of at least two parties to the concentration, realised by the sale of goods and/or services in the market of Bosnia and Herzegovina, amounts to at least BAM 8 million, according to the balance sheet for the financial year preceding the concentration, or if their common share in the relevant market exceeds 40%.

303. The total annual income referred to in paragraph 1 of Article 14 of the Law on Competition will not be calculated taking into account the incomes of all the parties to the concentration realised in their transactions.

304. In the case defined in Article 12, paragraph 1 of the Law on Competition, when the concentration consists in association or merger of a part or parts of one or more undertakings, irrespective whether or not those parts are constituted as legal entities, the calculation of the income within the meaning of paragraph 1 of the Article 14 of the Law on Competition, will include only the income deriving from the parts being the subject of the concentration control. If the case in question involves two or more concentrations conducted within a two-year period, it will be considered to constitute one concentration arising on the date of the last concentration.

I. The Calculation of Financial Threshold for Banks and Other Financial Institutions

305. Due to the specific nature of business that the banks and other financial institutions perform, the Law on Competition has specified a different way to calculate the threshold to report concentration. In line with that, Article 15 of the Law on Competition specifies that for the purpose of control of concentration in banks, other financial institutions and insurance companies, instead of the total turnover, the following shall be considered:

a. for legal persons which provide financial services, after deduction of the value added and other taxes directly related to them, the sum of the following income terms shall be used: interest income and similar incomes, income from securities and commissions, net profit on financial operations, and other operating income;
b. for the insurance companies and the companies which perform reinsurance activities, the value of gross premiums, which comprises all amounts received and receivable in respect of insurance contracts issued by or on behalf of the insurance company, including also reinsurance premiums, and after deduction of taxes and parafiscal contribution charged by reference to the amount of individual premiums or the total volume of premiums.

II. The Procedure of Notification of Concentration and the Adoption of the Decision on Its Permissibility

306. Article 16 of the Law on Competition determined the method and time limits for filing a notification. In line with that, undertakings-parties to the concentration are obliged to submit a notification of concentration within fifteen days of the conclusion of the agreement, the announcement of the public bid for shares or acquisition of controlling interest, depending on which action takes place first. The notification of concentration can also be filed when undertakings-parties to the concentration prove their intent for concentration with a closed principal agreement, memorandum of understanding or a letter of intent signed by all parties to the concentration or by public announcement of the intention of buying offer.

307. Pursuant to Article 17 of the Law on Competition, in making the assessment of intended concentration, the Council of Competition analyses the positive and negative effects, or whether that concentration creates or strengthens the dominant position which will result in the significant distortion of market competition, in particular: (a) the structure of the relevant market; (b) the effects of the concentration concerned on other actual and potential competitors; (c) the market position of parties in competition, their market shares, economic and financial power; (d) alternatives available to suppliers and users; (e) economic, legal and other barriers to entry to the market; (f) level of internal and international competitiveness of the parties to concentration; (g) supply and demand trends for the relevant goods and/or services; (h) the trends of technical and economic progress; (i) consumers' interests.

308. Pursuant to Article 18 of the Law on Competition, if the Council of Competition, when assessing the intended concentration, determines that the implementation of concentration might result in negative effects that can significantly disrupt the competition in the relevant market, it will make a decision to initiate proceedings.

309. Paragraph 2 of Article 18 of the Law on Competition stipulates the potential decisions/solutions of the Council of Competition, which: (a) assess the concentration concerned as compatible; (b) assess the concentration concerned as incompatible; (c) assess the concentration concerned as conditionally compatible, whereby measures, conditions and time limits are determined as well.

III. Other Relevant Notions

310. The intended concentration of economic entities is required to be notified by parties to the concentration, if the following conditions are met:

a. total annual income of all participants to the concentration achieved by selling goods and/or services on the world market is KM 100,000,000 according to the final account in the year preceding the concentration; and
b. total annual income of each of at least two economic entities – participants to the concentration realised by selling goods and/or services on the market of Bosnia and Herzegovina is at least KM 8,000,000 according to the final account in the year preceding the concentration, or if their joint share in the relevant market exceeds 40%.

The above-mentioned total annual income shall not include income that these economic entities achieve in mutual exchange.

311. In the case when the concentration related to a merger or acquisition of part or parts of one or more economic entities, irrespective of whether these parts have the status of legal entity, in calculating the income shall be calculated only the income of those parts of economic entity which are subject to the control of the concentration. Two or more concentrations referred to in the previous provision conducted within a period of less than two years shall be considered to constitute one concentration (more successive acquisitions of parts of an economic entity) implemented on the date of the last transaction.

312. Economic entities, participants in the concentration, are required to submit a notification of concentration within fifteen days of signing the agreement, the publication of public offering or acquisition of control, depending on what happens first. Notification of concentration may be filed when the participants to the concentration demonstrate their intention to concentrate by means of concluded agreement in principle, memorandum of understanding, letter of intent signed by all parties to the concentration or publication of intent to purchase.

313. In the case when control over the whole or parts of one or more economic entities is acquired by the other economic entity, the notification is to be submitted by economic entity acquiring control; in all other cases, economic entities shall submit a joint application.

314. Council of Competition is obliged to publish the data from the notification of concentration in daily newspapers, in particular:

a. the names of economic entities (the participants) in the concentration;

b. a form of concentration; and
c. the economic sector within the concentration takes place.

Council of Competition during the assessment of intended concentration analyses the effect which has resulted in significant distortion of market competition, or whether such concentration creates or strengthens a dominant position, and in particular:

a. the structure of the relevant market;
b. the effects of concentration on the other actual and potential competitors;
c. the position of the participants in the competition, their market shares, economic and financial powers;
d. the ability and choice of suppliers and customers;
e. economic, legal and other barriers to market entry;
f. levels of internal and international competitiveness of the participants in the concentrations;
g. trends of supply and demand of relevant goods and/or services;
h. trends of technical and economic development;
i. the interest of consumer.

§2. Structure of Proceedings

I. Preliminary Assessment and Full Investigation

315. Council of Competition following the receipt of the notification determines whether the notification is filed by an authorised person, whether it contains prescribed information and attachments, certified copies and translations into one of the official languages of Bosnia and Herzegovina. In the case that the applicant, for justified reasons, and despite the exerted efforts, is not able to collect certain data or documents of the compulsory contents of the notification, it will be written on the appropriate place of the notification, stating:

a. by whom and when the information or documents were tried to be obtained;
b. the reasons why the information or documents could not be collected;
c. where the Council of Competition can collect the missing information or documents.

The council of Competitions in the above-described case may ask the applicant to submit, in writing, instead of the missing data, his own analysis and assessment of conditions and situations to which the missing data pertains. The notification of concentration with all the data necessary shall be deemed to be a complete notification.

316. When it finds that notification is complete, the Council of Competition shall issue an acknowledgement to the applicant which particularly contains:

a. the number and issue date of the acknowledgement;
b. the name of the economic entity or the name of the applicant or authorised person;
c. the names of economic entities, the parties of the concentration;
d. the date of submission of the notification to the Council of Competition;
e. instructions that the concentration will not be implemented before the Council of Competition issues a decision which confirms the compatibility of concentration;
f. instruction that time limit shall commence on the basis of Articles 18 and 41 of the Act;
g. the signature of the President of the Council of Competition.

II. Right of Defence

317. Decisions of the Council of Competition are final and binding on the entire territory of Bosnia and Herzegovina and enforceable on the day of publication. Unsatisfied party to the proceedings may start administrative dispute before the Court of Bosnia and Herzegovina within thirty days of receipt of the decision, or from the date of publication of the decision.

III. Time Framework

318. The intended concentration of Economic entities must be notified by the parties to the concentration to the Council of Competitionin the manner prescribed in the Regulation on Notification and Criteria for Assessment of Concentration of Undertakings, within a period not exceeding one days from the date of signing contract/agreement, the publication of a public offer of shares or acquisition of control, depending on what occurs earlier.

319. The notification of concentration may be submitted to the Council of Competition after the participants have proven their intention to concentrate by conclusion of agreement in principle, memorandum of understanding, letter of intent or a public announcement of intent to bid purchase.

§3. Clearance and Conditional Clearance

I. Conditions and Undertakings

A. Timing

320. Council of Competition when assessing the intended concentration primarily analyses the effect that results in significant distortion of market competition. In the case that the Council of Competition, within thirty days from the date of issuance of an acknowledgement, does not issue a decision on initiation of proceedings for assessment of the concentration, concentration is deemed to be approved. In the case that decision on notification of concentration has not been issued within thirty days, the Council of Competition shall issue, at the request of the applicant, a decision declaring the concentration compatible.

321. The Council of Competition shall adopt one of the following decisions:

a. the concentration is compatible;
b. the concentration is not compatible;
c. the concentration is conditionally compatible.

Council of Competition when assessing that the concentration is conditionally compatible shall determine the extent, conditions and terms of their fulfilment.

322. The participants in the conditionally compatible concentration may continue the implementation of the concentration after filling out the measures and terms and conditions, unless the Council of Competition, due to particular justified request, determines different.

323. Council of Competition, on the basis of information and documentation that are submitted with the notification of concentration, the degree of probability of violation of competition rules through such concentration, and estimation that the intended concentration does not result in negative effects, may adopt a decision within thirty days.

324. In case the Council of Competition, within thirty days, starting from the date of issuance of the acknowledgement of receipt of complete and adequate notification, does not adopt a conclusion on initiation of the process of assessment of concentration, the concentration shall be deemed declared compatible. If the Council of Competition does not declare decision on concentration within three months, according to Article 41 of the Competition Act, concentration shall be deemed to be compatible.

325. Council of Competition may, ex officio or upon request of a party, amend the decision when the parties cannot fulfil certain conditions or when they infringe some of the measures set forth in the decision of the Council of Competition, owing to particular circumstances that could not be predicted or avoided and which do not depend on volition of the parties.

326. Concentrations shall not be implemented prior to the issuance of decision which confirms the compliance of the concentration concerned according to the Competition Act. The above-mentioned provision does not prevent the implementation of the public offering, which is reported to the competent authorities in accordance with the valid legislation, as well as activities which relate to acquisition of control over economic entities regulated by other laws.

§4. Relations with Other Merger Control Authorities

327. No other merger control authorities are prescribed by the Law of Bosnia and Herzegovina.

Chapter 3. Challenging the Administrative Decision

§1. Competent Courts

328. The competent court is the Court of Bosnia and Herzegovina. As the Competition Act prescribes, the decision of the Council of Competition is final. Unsatisfied party to the proceedings may start administrative dispute before the Court of Bosnia and Herzegovina within thirty days of receipt of the decision, or from the date of publication of the decision.

§2. Time Limits

329. The administrative dispute may be started before the Court of Bosnia and Herzegovina within thirty days of receipt of the decision, or from the date of publication of the decision.

§3. Scope of the Judicial Review

330. According to the Law on Administrative Disputes of Bosnia and Herzegovina (Official Gazette of Bosnia and Herzegovina, No. 19/02), the Court shall settle the dispute by judgment.

331. An action shall be approved or rejected as ungrounded. If the action is approved, the Court shall annul the disputed final administrative act.

332. The judgment shall annul the final administrative act and remand the case to the competent institution, or the final administrative act shall be annulled by the judgment and administrative matter shall be settled. Such judgment shall completely replace the disputed final administrative act. The judgment shall be and it can be disputed only by extraordinary legal remedies.

333. By the judgment annulling the final administrative act, the Court shall also decide on the request of the plaintiff on repossession of object or compensation of damages if the data on the procedure gives sound ground. Otherwise, if the issue is a more complex procedure (presentation of evidences, evaluation of documentation, etc.), the Court shall decide according to the provisions of the Law on Civil Procedure.

Selected Bibliography

Legal Sources

Code of Criminal Procedure of Bosnia and Herzegovina was imposed by the decision of the High Representative and published in the 'Official Gazette of BiH', No. 3/03.
Company Law of RS, 'The Official Gazette of the Republic of Srpska', No. 127/08.
Competition Act, 'The Official Gazette of BiH', Nos 48/05, 76/07, 80/09.
Constitution of Bosnia and Herzegovina.
Criminal Code of Bosnia and Herzegovina.
Criminal Code of FBiH.
Criminal Code of the Republic of Srpska.
Decision on Block Exemption Granted to Certain Categories of Vertical Agreements (between undertakings operating on the different level of production or distribution); 'The Official Gazette of BiH', No. 18/06.
Guide to The Yugoslav Legal System (1977), Institute of Comparative Law, Belgrade.
Law on Administrative Procedure, 'The Official Gazette of BiH', Nos 29/02, 12/04, 88/07 i 91/09.
Law on Companies of FBiH, 'The Official Gazette of the Federation of BiH', Nos 23/99, 45/00, 2/02, 6/02, 29/03, 68/05, 91/07, 84/08.
Law on Consumer Protection of BiH 'The Official Gazette of BiH', No. 25/06.
Law on Copyright and Related Rights and Law on the Collective Management of Copyright and Related Rights 'The Official Gazette of BiH', No. 63/10.
Law on Foreign Trade Policy of BiH 'The Official Gazette of BiH', No. 7/98.
Law on Public Enterprises in FBiH 'The Official Gazette of the Federation of BiH', Nos 08/05, 81/08.
Law on Public Enterprises in RS 'The Official Gazette of the Republic of Srpska', No. 75/04.
Law on the State Aid System 'The Official Gazette of BiH', No. 10/12
Law on Trade of FBiH, 'The Official Gazette of the Federation of BiH', Nos 64/04 i 12/05.
Law on Trade of RS, 'The Official Gazette of the Republic of Srpska', No. 6/ 07.
Patent Law of Bosnia and Herzegovina Official Gazette of BiH, No. 53/10.
Regulation on Agreements of Minor Importance 'The Official Gazette of BiH', No. 86/05.

Selected Bibliography

Regulation on Block Exemption Granted to Agreements on Distribution and Servicing of Motor Vehicles 'The Official Gazette of BiH', No. 16/06.

Regulation on Block Exemption Granted to Certain Categories of Horizontal Agreements (Between Undertakings Operating on the Same Level of Production or Distribution Chain) Relating Particularly to Research, Development and Specialisation Agreements 'The Official Gazette of BiH', No. 15/06.

Regulation on Block Exemption Granted to Certain Categories of Technology Transfer Agreements (Licence and Know-how Agreements); 'The Official Gazette of BiH', No. 15/06.

Regulation on Block Exemption Granted to Insurance Agreements; 'The Official Gazette of BiH', No. 15/06.

Regulation on Definition of a Dominant Position; 'The Official Gazette of BiH', No. 18/06.

Regulation on Notification and Criteria for the Assessment of a Concentration of Undertakings 'The Official Gazette of BiH', No. 34/10.

Regulation on the Procedure for Granting Immunity from Fines (Leniency Policy) 'The Official Gazette of BiH', No. 34/10.

The Ruling of the Constitutional Court; U 5/98-III.

Books and Articles

Kanita Imamović-Čizmić, Market Competition Legal Protection Mechanism in Bosnia and Herzegovina, LAP LAMBERT Academic Publishing (20 May 2014).

Branko Morait, Sloboda ugovaranja i pravo konkurencije u savremenoj sudskoj praksi, Pravna riječ, (36) Banja Luka, 2013.

Boris Mandić, 'Problem oligopola na tržištu telekomunijskijskih usluga u BiH', Mastrer rad, Miloš Trifković (2006), Određivanje monopolističkih sporazuma u pravima Bosne i Hercegovine i Evropske unije, Pregled, 4/2006, 91.

Bubalo Lana, (2013) Institut prinudne licence u međunarodnom, uporednom i bosanskohercehovačkom pravu, Nova pravna revija.

Others

Bosnia and Herzegovina, the Council of Competition of BiH, 'Annual Report on the Operations of the Council of Competition in 2012.'

Report on the Operations of the Council of Competition of Bosnia and Herzegovina in 2012.

'BILTEN' GASBiH Februar 2012, br. 23, Centar za politike i upravljanje, Izvještaj o politikama energetskog sektora u Bosni i Hercegovini, Septembar 2010.

Web

http://cbbh.ba/index.php?id=702&lang=hr.

Index

The numbers here refer to paragraph numbers.

www.ingramcontent.com/pod-product-compliance
Lightning Source LLC
Chambersburg PA
CBHW071353230926
51846CB00002B/537
* 9 7 8 9 4 0 3 5 6 3 6 0 2 *